Table of Contents

Introduction 9
    Children of Divorce 10
    Do I Stay or Do I Go? 11
    Impact of Children Staying in High Conflict Situations 11
    Successful Co-Parenting 12
    What We Will Cover 13

Chapter 1: Effects of Separation 15
    The Psychological Effects of Divorce on Children 16
    Divorce-Related Stress 17
    Effects of Divorce on Children 17
    Child Custody Battles 20
    Parent-Child Contact 21
    Impact of Custodial Arrangements on Children 21
    How to Minimize Children's Stress During Custodial Battles 23
    Signs Your Child Is Struggling 25
    Symptoms and Signs of Stress 25
    Reflective Questions 27
    Summary 28

Chapter 2: Co-Parenting for Your Child 29
    What Is a Co-Parenting Plan? 30
    How to Set Up a Co-Parenting Plan 31
    Additional Things to Consider 33
    Accept Your Individuality and Prioritize Your Child 35
    Work Together, Not Apart 36

Factors Which Can Increase Stress During or Post-Divorce 36
Supporting Children During Divorce 37
Early Intervention Programs 39
Tips for Reassuring Children 39
Quick Review of Successful Co-Parenting 42
Reflective Questions 42
Summary 43

Chapter 3: Building a Better Parent-Child Relationship .. 44
The Importance of Parent-Child Relationship 45
Examples of Positive Parenting 46
How to Improve a Parent-Child Relationship 48
Changes in Your Relationship After Divorce 54
Why Your Child Might Be Feeling Angry and Why They Are Taking it out on You 55
Working With Your Ex 56
When Your Ex Will Not Cooperate 57
What to Do if You Feel Like Your Child Hates You 57
Child Discipline 59
Deciding on Discipline in Co-Parenting Situations 61
Quick Tips for Effective Discipline in a Co-Parenting Situation .. 63
Common Mistakes in Discipline With a Co-Parent 64
Reflective Questions 64
Summary 65

Chapter 4: The Toxic Co-Parent 66
Signs You Are Dealing With a Toxic Co-Parent 68
How a Toxic Parent Raises Their Children 72
How Toxic Parents Affect Children's Mental Health 74

Co-Parenting With a Toxic Ex

Tips and Strategies to Set Boundaries, Cope With Parental Alienation, and Manage Conflicts Without Losing Your Mind

Tiffany Austin

© Copyright 2023 – Tiffany Austin - All rights reserved

The content within this book may not be reproduced, duplicated, or transmitted without direct written permission from the author or publisher.

Under no circumstances will any blame or legal responsibility be held against the publisher, or author, for any damages, reparation, or monetary loss due to the information contained within this book, either directly or indirectly.

Legal Notice

This book is copyright protected. It is for personal use only. You cannot amend, distribute, sell, use, quote, or paraphrase any part, or the content within this book, without the author's or publisher's consent.

Disclaimer Notice

Please note that the information contained within this document is for educational and entertainment purposes only. All effort has been executed to present accurate, up-to-date, and reliable, complete information. No warranties of any kind are declared or implied. Readers acknowledge that the author is not engaging in rendering legal, financial, medical, or professional advice.

Dealing With a Toxic Co-Parent 77

Sticking to Your Boundaries 79

Empowering Others in the Co-Parenting Journey 83

Reflective Questions 85

Summary 85

Chapter 5: Parallel Parenting 86

What Is Parallel Parenting? 87

Co-Parenting Versus Parallel Parenting 88

How Does Successful Parallel Parenting Benefit Children? 88

Benefits of Parallel Parenting 88

How to Create a Parallel Parenting Plan 90

Tips for Successful Parallel Parenting 91

Parallel Parenting With a Toxic Co-Parent 93

Keys to Successfully Parallel Parenting With a Toxic Parent: 93

Parenting With an Uncooperative Parent 96

Is Your Ex Uncooperative or Just Difficult? 96

Potential Areas of Conflict and How to Manage 97

How to Handle an Uncooperative Parallel Parent 98

Reflective Questions 101

Summary 102

Chapter 6: Loyalty Conflicts 103

What is a Loyalty Conflict? 104

What Causes a Loyalty Conflict? 106

Early Warning Signs of Loyalty Conflicts 108

How Loyalty Conflicts Affect Children 111

How to Avoid Loyalty Conflicts 113

Loyalty Bind Talks With Children 116

 Additional Examples of Ways to Reassure Children 117

 Reflective Questions... 117

 Summary 118

Chapter 7: Parental Alienation 119

 What is Parental Alienation? 121

 Parental Alienation Versus Estrangement................................ 121

 Types of Alienating Parents 124

 When Does Parental Alienation Happen? 125

 Techniques That Parental Alienators Use................................ 126

 Signs of Children Experiencing Parental Alienation 131

 Effects of Parental Alienation on Children 132

 How to Protect Your Child Against Parental Alienation............. 134

 What NOT to Do if You Find Yourself on the Receiving End of Parental Alienation 136

 Involving the Court 138

 Reintegration Therapy 141

 How to Heal From Parental Alienation 141

 Looking After Yourself 142

 Reflective Questions... 143

 Summary 144

Chapter 8: What to Do When 145

 When Your Ex Refuses Access 147

 Why Your Ex Might Be Withholding Visitation......................... 148

 What to Do if Your Ex Is Not Following Your Parenting Plan....149

 Court Involvement 150

 Limited Contact... 151

 When Your Ex Is Badmouthing You 152

Types of Badmouthing 153
How Badmouthing Affects Children 154
How to Respond to Badmouthing.. 155
Tips for Dealing With Badmouthing... 156
Responding to Negative Communication From Your Ex 158
Dealing With Arguments 159
Improving Communication.. 159
Communication Quick Tips 161
When Your Ex Sabotages Your Parenting Time 161
How to Handle a Co-Parent Who Is Not Following the Plan 162
Stepparents and New Partners 163
If You Feel Like Your Ex Is Trying to Replace You 163
How to Co-Parent With New Partners... 164
Introducing a New Partner to Your Children 165
How Does the Court View New Partners? 166
"My Kids Hate My New Partner!"... 167
How to Respond to Children Rejecting Your New Partner 167
When Your Ex Undermines Your Authority................................170
How to Respond to an Ex Undermining Your Authority............ 171
Are You Undermining Your Authority? 172
When Your Ex Manipulates Your Child....................................... 173
How to Respond to Your Ex Manipulating Your Children 173
When Your Ex Harasses You 174
Types of Harassment.. 175
When Your Ex Cyberbullies You 176
When You Feel Like Your Child is Abandoning You for Their Other Parent 176

When Your Child Refuses Visitation 178
When Your Child Feels Ashamed 180
What to Do if Your Child Is Struggling 181
Reflective Questions 183
Summary 184
A Heartfelt Request 185
Conclusion 186
About the Author 187
References 189

Introduction

"It is easier to build strong children than repair broken men."

— Frederick Douglass

Like most people, I was pretty naive. My wedding was the happiest day of my life. Walking down the aisle, I was sure that I was set for life. We were unstoppable. We could resolve any fight, conquer any slip-up, and come back from any breakdown. We were a team, a unit. This feeling only intensified when my daughter was born. This little breakable creature in the big, wide world. We were her protectors. Unfortunately, not every fairytale ends in a happily ever after. It turns out that "I do" does not mean "I will, forever." As much as you think you know someone inside out, it also turns out that people can be harboring a great deal more inside of themselves that they are not showing you.

I learned this the hard way, and I am still learning how to navigate life after "this is not working." Learning how to co-parent with someone so different from the person whom I walked down the aisle and agreed to marry still challenges me every day. How do you share responsibility for your child, whom you love more than anything else in the world, with a stranger? Especially when that stranger is using all the vulnerabilities you shared with them in your time together against you? Playing happy families after separation is not impossible, but it feels like an urban myth for many. Through *sharing this book, I am hoping I can share some of the lessons I have learned in how to parent alongside someone who seemingly does not always have your child's best interests at heart.*

Children of Divorce

Perhaps surprisingly, overall rates of divorce in America are falling. Nonetheless, around 35% of all marriages in the US end in divorce, equal to about 2.5 per 1,000 total population (CDC, 2000-2021). Of this, between 8-15% of divorces are classified as 'high conflict,' meaning that the separation is far from amicable (Kelly, 2003). Divorce proceedings in high-conflict cases will often involve lengthy legal battles lasting between 2-3 years, oftentimes throughout the entirety of their children's early lives.

Divorce and separation also have significant negative impacts on children's livelihoods. Initial behavioral issues may include emotional distress, feelings of abandonment, bed-wetting, anger, and insecurity. Children of divorce are more likely to engage in aggression and behavioral issues, and less likely to demonstrate pro-social behaviors. They are two times more likely to be at or below the poverty line in later life (D'Onofrio, Emery, 2019), and engage in drug use or other problematic behaviors.

A disrupted childhood also impacts scholastic success, with estimates that children of divorce are 8% less likely to complete high school, 12% less likely to attend college, and 11% less likely to finish college (Brand, Moore, Song, Xie, 2003).

Do I Stay or Do I Go?

Reviewing the above statistics can be incredibly distressing, as it is natural to want nothing but the best for your children. Starting them off several steps behind what you envision as children from happy, nuclear families to be can be guild-inducing. More often than not, I have been left wondering whether I should have stuck it out and stayed in my marriage; sought more options, tried more therapists, and given it my all. Should we stay together for the sake of the kids? But by the time it ended, I had already given it my all. I was at a breaking point, and I had already exhausted every option.

Impact of Children Staying in High Conflict Situations

The sad reality is that children from high-conflict homes, with parents still actively engaging in fights daily, suffer just as much emotional distress as those from divorced parents - if not more. Calling it a day and going your separate ways is often the best solution for everyone involved. As isolating as a divorce or separation process may feel, know that you are not alone in this. I too was amongst those who felt lost and hopeless after the initial proceedings of my divorce. All the years I had spent building up my family, my team, and my unit, were gone with one signature. Years of my life were wiped away. Part of me wanted to wallow and hibernate, with a pint of ice cream in one hand and a bottle of wine in the other. However, I had my daughter to think about. I could cry in private, but I had to find a way to present myself as strong and certain and pave out new ways to parent a child who was living between two homes. This often meant crying in the car, at the grocery store – once, embarrassingly, at the gym. Whilst dealing with the downfall of my marriage, I was also dealing with an ex-partner who seemed out to get me. I was constantly barraged by texts and calls, had shouting matches in the driveway, and clashes on parent's night.

The first year is after all the hardest. However, we found a way through it. Or I did, rather, largely working against someone who would always double down when it came to organizing who would have our daughter on weekends or would drive her to after-school classes. Someone whom I at one point considered my person, my best friend, my partner in crime, suddenly worked against me when it came to the most important task we both had; raising our daughter.

Successful Co-Parenting

The idea of parenting with someone you are no longer together with is a daunting one, even more so when you do not get along with that person. However, it is not impossible. It works for many. To name a few of the celebrities who live in the limelight, Adele and her ex-husband Konecki, who divorced in 2016. Kourtney Kardashian and Scott Disick, never formally got married but have co-parented post-separation. Chris Martin and Gwyneth Paltrow, who coined the term 'conscious uncoupling' for their 2015 divorce and have continued to share joint custody and co-parent their children. Many of these celebrities claim co-parenting to be an easy dream, which may or not be the case. They also have access to nannies, therapists, and far more resources than the average parent might. However, in most cases, parents can and will find a way to navigate parenting after separation.

What We Will Cover

Whilst putting your differences aside may not be an option, and you might still feel far off from the success the celebrity examples above claim to have found, this book imparts certain approaches you can use to navigate your new life. I have condensed what took me several years to learn into this book, to assist and guide you in learning new methods for how to deal with co-parenting, particularly with a toxic co-parent. By the end of this book, you will be familiar with numerous approaches and techniques which you can instill into your daily life.

This book will equip you with the basis of many proven methods for managing the following:

- Understanding the effects of separation and divorce on children

- Understanding the basic premise of co-parenting and how to do so successfully

- How to build and improve upon a parent-child relationship

- How to spot a toxic co-parent

- Parallel parenting, for when co-parenting fails, and how to do so effectively

- How to manage loyalty and resentment within a child growing up in two homes

- How to deal with parental alienation from a toxic ex

- Potential solutions for scenarios that might arise when dealing with a toxic and difficult co-parent

The process is not a one-size-fits-all. A large portion of building your new life and finding what works for you also involves trial and error. However, stumbling blindly in the dark and failing to try new tactics will prolong stages of conflict and strife, oftentimes meaning that your children also remain in conflict-heavy surroundings for longer periods.

The outcome of a successful and happy co-parenting situation looks different for everyone, and with the help of the guidelines, methods, and approaches in this book, we will work to make your transition into co-parenting as smooth as possible and minimize this conflict and stress upon your children during the process.

Whilst a future in which you can communicate calmly with your ex and discuss various parenting approaches might currently seem like a far-off ideal, building a healthy relationship with an ex is not impossible. By creating an individual parenting plan, continuing to prioritize the well-being of your children, and learning to maintain strict boundaries, you can also look to a future in which parenting with an ex will work for you.

Chapter 1:
Effects of Separation

"The best security blanket a child can have is parents who respect each other." — Jan Blaustone

Taking the leap and deciding to separate for good is a big step. It is also a brave step, as many couples refrain from doing so - with one study estimating that 1 in 4 married couples stay together in unhappy marriages only for the sake of their children (Irwin Mitchell, 2014). It is also not an easy decision to make, particularly if you have children with the individual you are divorcing. However, the decision to divorce or separate is often not a sudden one, and is generally broken up into the following stages over several years before the actual divorce:

1. Initial Doubts (usually initiated by one party):
   - Increased conflict and arguments
   - Resentment
   - Increased feelings of distance

2. Expressing Unhappiness:
   - Verbalizing dissatisfaction
   - Potential counseling
   - Potential attempt at rekindling

3. Deciding to Divorce/Separate:
   - Increased emotional distance
   - High chances of extramarital affairs
   - Tension and resentment

4. Separation:
   - Physical separation/divorce
   - Re-establishing self
   - Involving legal proceedings if necessary
   - Dividing mutual friends and loved ones
   - Navigating parenting post-separation

The Psychological Effects of Divorce on Children

The first year after a separation or divorce is often the hardest for children. They struggle with coming to terms with the immense change and upheaval in their lives and likely experience a range of emotions, from anger and resentment to fear and insecurity. However, most children do grow to accept and adapt to their new living arrangements.

The effects of divorce and separation vary amongst children of different ages, and are generally broken up accordingly:

- Young children (2-8 years) will have difficulty in understanding the changes in their lives, and the reasons behind them having to travel between two homes.

- School-age children (8-12 years) may blame themselves for the divorce, and harbor feelings of shame and guilt over having caused their parents to split.
- Teenagers (13-18 years) might become increasingly angry toward one or both parents for the divorce, and resent them for breaking up the family.

Divorce-Related Stress

Big changes bring with them a great deal of stress for many children who find comfort in routines and schedules. Changing schools, having to make new friends, moving to a new home, and often having to adapt to a different style of living due to financial hardships can all be potential stressors for children of divorce.

Additionally, parent-child relationships will experience heightened tension. In many cases of separation, one parent assumes a greater allocation of the parenting responsibilities and may feel increasingly burdened and stressed by having to be a primary caregiver. Single mothers in particular are reported to be less supportive and affectionate towards their children post-divorce (Wallerstein, Lewis, Packer Rosenthal, 2013). Children tend also to feel less bonded to the parent they see less, (Anderson, 2014) which is most often their father figure.

Effects of Divorce on Children

Divorce can have an extensive negative impact on children. It is worth educating yourself on potential effects so that you can keep an eye out for these, even if they do not seem to apply to your current situation.

- Mental Health Problems:
  Children who struggle with the effects of divorce tend to be at an increased risk of psychological issues, leading to higher rates of symptoms that include: anxiety, sadness, guilt, feelings of worthlessness, depression, fatigue, weight gain or weight loss, restlessness, insomnia, or oversleeping.

- Poor Academic Performance:
  The academic success rates of children from divorced or separated homes are considerably lower than that of children from intact families, due to a mixture of factors including children being distracted from school due to the ongoings at home. Grades tend to be lower, and dropout rates higher, often accompanied by lower educational aspirations.

- Behavioral Problems and Substance Abuse:
  An increase in risk-taking behaviors such as early and increased usage of substances like tobacco, marijuana, and alcohol has been seen to be prevalent among children from divorced families. Additionally, children whose parents divorced when they were aged 5 or under tend to be at a higher risk of becoming sexually active before the age of 6 and engaging with a higher number of sexual partners during their teenage years (Donahue, D'Onofrio, Bates, Lansford, Dodge, Pettit, 2010).

- Reduced Interest in Socializing:
  A lack of trust in their friends, irritability, and other negative feelings can leave children of divorce or separation less willing to engage with friends or other social behaviors. They may feel isolated, as if they are the only individual going through such a situation, and subsequently cut themselves off further from those around them.

- Struggling to Adapt:
  Divorce and separation bring with them huge changes and upheaval in the life of a child. Many children experience heightened forms of the effects mentioned above when having to come to terms with changes in their lives, such as new living situations, new family dynamics, change of school, and having to find new friends.

- Guilt:
  Particularly among young children, some may blame themselves for the divorce, and struggle to understand why their parents no longer love each other. This will again contribute to an increase in negative feelings of self-worth.

- Struggling With Adult Romantic Relationships and Marriage:
  Watching their parents fall out of love and choose to separate can lead to children experiencing difficulties when it comes to forming romantic relationships. Feelings of fear of abandonment and lack of trust can limit their ability to form

bonds later in life and often leads to disillusionment when it comes to marrying themselves. There is also a higher likelihood that children of divorce will experience divorce themselves in adulthood.

- Increase in Health Problems:
Increased stress levels throughout the divorce process have been linked to a rise in physical health issues, such as migraines, digestive issues, and an overall compromised immune system.

Child Custody Battles

Child custody battles can be lengthy procedures, which can be drawn out into nasty fights and attacks upon character if one or both parties deem the other unfit for parenting. Prolonged legal battles can be immensely damaging to the well-being of children, and custody outcomes vary. Different types of child custody include:

- Legal Custody:

This can be split into sole legal custody, where one parent is entitled to make decisions relating to healthcare, education, and other important factors, or joint legal custody, where both parents share input into these factors.

- Physical Custody:

As above, sole physical custody will mean that one parent will largely physically house and raise the child, with limited visitation periods organized for the other parent. Joint physical custody involves the child moving between both homes as physical custody is shared.

Parent-Child Contact

In all custody cases, parent-child contact is impacted in one way or another. Studies have shown that in cases where mothers hold sole custody, visitation from fathers tended to increase over the years (Maccoby, Buchanan, Mnookin, Dornbusch, 1993). In comparison, in cases where fathers held sole custody, mothers tended to visit more.

Impact of Custodial Arrangements on Children

Custody arrangements may vary from case to case, and might often be outside of your control. It is still worth considering how your setup could impact your children, and how you can minimize any negative effects that could potentially arise.

- Sole Versus Joint Custody:

Although custody arrangements vary, the majority of research has found no significant difference in stress between children in sole physical custody versus joint physical custody (Augustijn, 2022). However, this can vary in every situation. In some sole custody scenarios, children may feel a certain level of guilt for not being able to spend as much time with the parent who holds secondary custody.

- Parental Hostility and Conflict:

Whilst adequate custodial setups can provide children with structured living situations, post-divorce parental conflict levels tend to be the factor that most contribute to the stress and negative impacts upon children of divorce. Whilst a child might routinely spend Monday to Thursday with mom, Friday to Sunday with dad, have their bedroom in each house, and lack any irregularity in their schedule, mom and dad still actively waging wars even post-divorce can lead to increased consequences including depression, substance abuse, and other forms of problematic behavior.

- Resident Parent's Gender:

Older studies suggest that boys benefit from growing up in the custody of their fathers, and girls benefit greater from growing up with their mothers. However, newer research has since shown vastly mixed results, from which it can be deemed that children do not receive any notable benefit from growing up with a parent of the same sex.

- Transitioning Between Households:

Joint custody situations may cause children stress because of feeling like they lack a concrete home, particularly if they have to spend a great deal of time traveling between the houses of both parents. However, children have also been deemed to adapt to these transitions, and in some cases even enjoy having two houses to call home.

How to Minimize Children's Stress During Custodial Battles

Custodial battles can be an incredibly stressful time for any children involved. Consider how to best mitigate any factors that might be stressors to your child, to best support them during this period.

- Avoid Discussing Divorce With Children:

It might be tempting to try and discuss the divorce, and your frustrations, and try to gauge what your ex is thinking through using your children as go-betweens between the both of you. However, children should be left out of divorce and separation proceedings as much as possible, as they may otherwise feel stressed, anxious, and pressured to side with one parent over the other or feel guilty for not doing so. Keep your annoyances to yourself as much as possible and maintain a safe and neutral space for your children.

- Do Not Use Children as Messengers:

Following on from the above, it can be tempting to tell your child to relay certain pieces of information to your ex. "Well, you can tell daddy there is no way he is going to be keeping the car", or "You know I am much better at Christmas dinners. Tell her that you want to be with me on Christmas, will you?" Your children should remain as removed from the situation as much as possible and feel in no way pressured to relay your anger or wishes, or spy on their other parent for you.

- Avoid Criticizing Their Other Parent:

It might be tempting to speak out about how vexed you are with your ex, and quite how much they are irritating you. Keep venting for people in your circle that you trust and can confide in, rather than name-calling in the presence of your children, or letting your anger get the better of you and confiding in them how much of a let-down their other parent is. Criticizing their other parent can cause a great deal of emotional duress that will only worsen tension during a divorce.

- Do Not Prevent Children From Seeing Their Other Parent or Try to Claim Them for Yourself Alone:

Growing up in the presence of both parents tends to prove far more valuable than growing up solely with one parent unless that parent is severely incapable of parenting due to issues such as drug problems or anger management. As difficult as it may feel, avoid claiming the children as yours and yours alone, and try to accept ways to allow for the presence of both parents in their lives.

- Do Not Use the Children to Your Advantage:

Leveraging your children to get what you want in a divorce should heavily be avoided. This includes encouraging them to state that they prefer living with you or asking them to criticize their other parent. Weaponizing your children only intensifies conflict and stress levels for everyone involved.

- Allow for Outside Input, Including From Friends and Family (to a degree), but Largely From Legal Representation:

Cutting costs by representing yourself in a legal battle will likely lead to no good. Allow input from your family and friends over plowing ahead by yourself, but also make sure to find lawyers with high success rates who are willing to take the time to listen to your case and assess your needs.

Signs Your Child Is Struggling

During a divorce, you might well be blindsided by everything else going on in your life, with all of your focus on the divorce and how it is proceeding. However, it is critical that you monitor your child, and keep a lookout for any early warning signs that they are experiencing high levels of stress as a result of the divorce or separation. Early intervention upon detecting these signs can mean less damage down the line.

Symptoms and Signs of Stress

Stress manifests in all different ways. Below are some of the most common examples of how stress manifests in children.

- Sadness:
  Increased sadness and crying, even over issues that seem unrelated to the divorce, can be a sign that your child is feeling overwhelmed and struggling to cope. This can lead to an inability to cope with even minor issues such as schoolwork or

chores and may seem to come out of nowhere.

- Anxiety and Worrying:
Sudden insecurities and worrying over issues that are unrelated to the divorce, such as attending school, socializing, or engaging in hobbies they previously enjoyed can demonstrate heightened stress levels. Children may need increased reassurance and care to help them deal with these worries.

- Withdrawing:
Some children will deal with the stress of divorce by withdrawing from daily life, and recluse to themselves. They may no longer engage in conversation, head straight up to their bedrooms and shut themselves away quietly, or refuse to socialize with their friends.

- Questioning Authority and Arguing:
Equally, children may show signs of stress by talking back and arguing, both at home and at school. A decreased inability to manage their temper or to engage with instructions can reflect difficulties in dealing with the divorce.

- Declining School Performance:
A decline in grades and schoolwork is also indicative of children experiencing difficulties in concentrating at school due to having issues surrounding their family life on their

minds. They may no longer feel like they care about their school performance, or feel increasingly stressed as they begin to perform poorly academically.

- Physical Symptoms:
  Headaches, migraines, nausea, gastrointestinal issues, and an overall impacted immune system can all be signs that stress is causing the manifestation of physical symptoms.

- Changes in Eating Habits:
  Stress can also lead to decreased or increased eating habits. This can develop further into eating disorders, or overeating as a form of emotional support.

- Changes in Sleep Patterns:
  Excessive sleep or sudden insomnia can both be indicators of increased stress levels. Some children may also experience sleep disturbances, such as nightmares or night terrors.

- Refusing to Spend Time With a Parent:
  Children may blame one parent for the entirety of the divorce and their heightened stress, and refuse to engage with them at all.

Reflective Questions

1. *Think about some ways you can best support a child who is showing signs of increased stress during or after a divorce. How*

might you let them know that you are there for them, even if they do not want to talk about it?
2. *Your child comes to your house and expresses that their other parent has criticized you over the weekend. How might you keep your cool and respond to these accusations?*
3. *You feel overwhelmed by anger after hearing about some of the expectations your ex has set out in the divorce. Who else might you turn to, to vent some of these frustrations?*

Summary

In this chapter, we have covered the initial process of divorce or separation, the different types of child custody, and the effects of divorce on children.

If you have not yet decided to separate, you have hopefully gained some key insight into different types of child custody and their effects on children, which might make you feel more at ease or help you in deciding what arrangement best fits you.

If you are already at or past that stage, you will have learned about the effects of divorce on children, and how to detect early signs of stress to help support their well-being throughout the process.

In the next chapter, you will learn about life *after* divorce or separation; methods for navigating parenting with an ex-partner effectively which work to keep the well-being of your children a priority.

Chapter 2:
Co-Parenting for Your Child

"There is no such thing as a "broken family." Family is family and is not determined by marriage certificates, divorce papers, and adoption documents. Families are made in the heart."

— C. JoyBell C.

*B*reakups are pretty hard. From my teens to my late twenties, I remember feeling deflated and inconsolable, with each breakup feeling like the end of the world. Looking back, however, going no-contact and never hearing from your ex again (apart from perhaps a late-night drunken text you are bound to regret in the morning), seems like a fever dream compared to what happens when you break up with someone with whom you share a child. Block, delete, and move on is not an option. You cannot just delete their number, erase your pictures together, or quietly un-tag yourself from social media posts. You have to find a way to move forward and connect your life in new ways. Acting as if they never existed in a desperate attempt to gain closure is off the cards. You keep their number saved (maybe having deleted the heart emojis adorning their name). You might keep a few pictures of you as a family, even if stashed away in a drawer somewhere. You have to find a way to heal even despite seeing their name pop up on your phone at frequent intervals throughout the week, whilst hearing *their voice on the other end of the phone, or whilst seeing them in person when dropping off your children. The conversations might be mundane; what time on Friday will you be around to pick her up? Did she leave her math book at your house? What are you thinking of getting her for Christmas this year? There is probably more you want to say, words left unspoken, and things you wish you had said sooner.*

The biggest part of navigating co-parenting is putting your child first. It is turning the communication you shared with your partner into words you might expect to hear in a boardroom. You sit at the board table, opposite someone you used to share a bed with, and set out goals, expectations, and targets. You learn how to negotiate, how to trade, how to deal professionally with slip-ups, and how to plan for even the most unlikely of situations. The journey into co-parenting is a transition from lovers to business partners and is not an easy one without rigorous organization.

What Is a Co-Parenting Plan?

Setting clear communication, expectations, and boundaries is a necessity for any healthy relationship. That also includes a successful parenting relationship with your ex (even if romance is no longer involved). As you will no longer be living side by side with your ex, and probably do not want to be in too regular in-person communication with them, setting out a co-parenting plan is an ideal way to set objectives for parenting. This can be done in court, through an outside mediator, or multiple modern resources including apps or joint calendars. It should cover all bases of what you both expect, how you will communicate, allocation of who is looking after your child when, and contingency plans should anything go wrong.

If it does not work out perfectly the first time around, it is also not the end of the world. You can continue to adapt your parenting plan as you go.

How to Set Up a Co-Parenting Plan

Work with your co-parent to set up a comprehensive parenting plan covering all aspects of childcare and your future relationship.

- Communication:
  Post-breakup, it is usually tempting to go no-contact and work on closure. However, with children involved, this tends not to be a viable option. Try and set out a clear communication plan in co-parenting with outlined methods such as whether you will use texting, phone calls, emails, or other communication methods. Set out what is and is not acceptable; for example, no late-night calls, or messages unrelated to childcare. Having a clear structure will often reduce conflict, as both parents know what level of communication to give and expect, and will reduce the risk of having to involve legal proceedings. Refrain also from using your children as messengers, to relay your feelings or requests, as this can lead to them feeling overburdened and stressed.

- Legal Custody:
Generally, after your divorce or separation, a clear custodial arrangement will have been set out. This will have deemed which parent holds decision authority when it comes to important decisions like which school your child will be attending and their medical care. A co-parenting plan can also outline this between themselves; for example, one parent is responsible for healthcare, and the other for education.

- Living Arrangements:
Perhaps the most defining factor of a co-parenting plan is where and when the children will be with each parent. This typically will involve two separate homes and a structured time set between each home. However, various other ways exist to set up living arrangements post-divorce or separation. Some parents decide that the children will reside mainly with one parent, and some other parents decide to continue living in the same house. Whatever the finalized setup, making sure that the two separate residences are not hugely far apart is usually a key factor for a smoother transition between households.

- Parent Time:
The time allocated to each parent to spend with their children will depend on the outcome of the physical custodial arrangements, and will also be dependent on visitation

schedules. Schedules should be set out, taking into account school time and employment of the parents. Planning key dates like birthdays and holidays far in advance, and rotating those when applicable, tends also to lead to reduced conflict about questions like who will have the kids over Christmas.

- Finances:

    Financial arrangements such as child support may have been set out in a court-ordered arrangement, but adding a section of your co-parenting plan that includes additional expenses can minimize conflict. Rigorously keeping track of all related expenses is also key, and can be done through shared documents or other modern resources.

Additional Things to Consider

Co-parenting plans are generally most successful when all possibilities are covered, and no situation is unplanned. Consider these additional aspects when formulating your plan to avoid conflict down the line.

- Cancellations:

Have a plan ready in case either parent, for whatever reason, needs to cancel their visitation time. Be mindful that life happens and last-minute cancellations will no doubt arise, so allow leniency for these occasions. However, be cautious if this becomes a regular occurrence, refer to Chapters 4 and 5 on how to deal with an uncooperative co-parent.

- Education:

Outline the expectations of both parents in terms of school choices, fees, extracurricular activities, and how best to support your children in their studies such as tutoring or homework.

- Healthcare:

Make sure that both parents are aware of where the child's doctor is, whether or not they are insured, and what to do in case of an emergency.

- Religion and Culture:

Discussing expectations if you or your ex are religious and want your children to also be involved in certain aspects is critical. This also applies to certain cultural influences.

- Travel:

Whilst holiday time should be set out and agreed upon in advance, you might request that your partner notify you if they want to take your child abroad. Whilst it is fair to ask to be told what your child is getting up to abroad, refrain from being overbearing or restrictive. Co-parenting also involves a great deal of trust and confidence that your co-parent will make the right decisions when it comes to your children.

- Childcare:

Children tend to work best with regular and consistent routines. Staying up until midnight at one parent's house, and having to go to bed at 8 p.m. with the other will no doubt lead to arguments. Try to set out expectations for things such as how much screen time your child is allowed, at what age they might be allowed their phone, how long they should spend on their homework, and how to discipline them if they misbehave.

- Additional Involvement:

Formalize an agreement of any additional childcare requirements like babysitting, and who will care for the children in case of events like a sickness. Also communicate if additional individuals might be involved in childcare, like grandparents and new partners.

- Conflict Resolution:

In case of disagreements, and to avoid increased conflict and stress upon both parents and children, having a plan in place when conflict does arise is key. This might involve a mediator or even a court.

Accept Your Individuality and Prioritize Your Child

The above suggestions might not apply to everyone. Every family is different, particularly post-separation. You know yourself and your child best, and it is key that you incorporate their best interests into your co-parenting plan. This might even sometimes come at a cost to you –they want to spend the summer with their other parent, whose family has a house near the beach. Are you going to put your foot down and demand that they spend their allocated time with you, or are you going to take your child's desires into account? Whilst you are indeed the adult and the guardian in your relationship with your child, this does also require at times, putting your demands aside if you feel that it is in your child's best interest.

Work Together, Not Apart

Whilst your divorce or separation might have felt like a battle, co-parenting is not a case of winning or losing. The more you cooperate, generally, the more successful your co-parenting relationship will be. There will undoubtedly be periods of strife and friction at the start of a co-parenting plan, however, try where possible to work together and communicate through these issues to strengthen your setup. Attending therapy, when possible, will also help you navigate some of the difficult feelings associated with early co-parenting struggles.

Factors Which Can Increase Stress During or Post-Divorce

Be mindful of things that can heighten stress for children during a divorce, and if you find that the following apply to your situation, consider how you might be able to improve them or discuss them with your child.

- High conflict situations, arguing, tension, and abuse
- Numerous changes, for example moving house, moving

school, remarriage
- Decreased parental attention
- Parental mental health issues
- Change in the economic situation

Supporting Children During Divorce

In the previous chapter, we covered some of the symptoms children who are experiencing stress due to divorce might display. Below are methods you can use to comfort them and support them through these issues. However, if you feel that they are in any way suffering more than expected, do seek out professional support.

- Guilt:

For children experiencing guilt and blaming themselves for the divorce, be sure that you and your ex communicate how this is not at all their fault, and that you still both love them regardless of the separation.

- Anxiety:

Huge changes and upheavals in a child's life can cause sudden anxiety, which might manifest in excessive worrying, regression, or other nervous behaviors. Establishing consistency can help put children at ease in their new situations, as can repeated verbal reassurance.

- Behavioral Issues:

Anxiety and overwhelming thoughts can also manifest in sudden acting up or behavioral changes. Creating firm boundaries and being present to talk through your child's struggles can help reduce some of these behaviors. However, if you think that they are at all at risk, do seek professional help. Make sure you are also on the same page as your co-parent when it comes to creating boundaries and enacting discipline.

- Withdrawing:

Whilst some children respond to stress through acting out, others withdraw from activities they enjoyed previously and will spend more time on their own. Try, where possible, to encourage their participation in social and recreational activities, but be mindful of the fact that they might be struggling to adjust. Also be conscious that excessive withdrawal may also be a sign of depression, and may require escalation to professional help.

- Poor Academic Performance:

Lower grades can be a sign of struggling to concentrate at school. Children going through a divorce have a lot on their minds. Be mindful of this, but try to encourage open communication, support, and a routine when it comes to academic events like homework. It is also worth mentioning your divorce to the school, so they are also aware of your child's mindset and can also adapt to support them best.

Early Intervention Programs

There are various models which have been clinically proven to enhance the coping skills of both children and parents during and post-divorce. Amongst these, is the Children of Divorce Intervention Program (CODIP). This is a support group session program for second and third-grade children, which helps them feel less isolated, to understand the reasons for divorce better, and teaches them coping skills for divorce-related stress.

The eNew Beginnings Program (eNBP) is an outpatient program for children aged 3 to 18. It aims to teach parents tools to help improve family relationships through learning effective listening tools, and how to establish effective boundaries and discipline methods. It also assists children in learning how to manage their anger and is delivered over ten sessions for up to eight parents.

Additionally, 17 states require court-mandated divorce education for parents post-divorce, as research has demonstrated so many benefits from attending these classes.

Tips for Reassuring Children

In addition to your parenting plan, think ahead when it comes to how you can best support your child during or after a divorce.

- Be Prepared:

Children may come with a list of concerns and worries about how their lives are going to change after the divorce. Be prepared to have a calm and reassuring answer to all questions like "Where will I live?" "Who is going to take me to school?" and "What is going to happen to our family dog?"

Being able to reassure children that you have a plan ready for all big life changes, and an answer to everything will make them feel more comfortable and supported throughout the transition. They might be a little scared by all these changes, but they can trust you to ferry them through it all.

- Minimize Changes:

Where possible, minimize the number of changes that children will experience. This might not always be achievable, however, maintaining the same schedule, the same school, and the same neighborhood, can greatly reduce the stress experienced by other vast changes.

- Reassurance:

Reassure your child that you love them. Even if they seem unwilling to engage or respond, regular verbal reassurance can go a long way, as can other acts of devotion such as picking up their favorite snack or taking them on a trip out. Equally, if their co-parent fails to show up or lets them down, try to reassure your child that they are still loved by both parents.

- Listen and Create a Safe Space for Hidden Emotions:

Equally, if your child does feel let down by you or your co-parent, create a safe space in which they can voice these concerns. Demonstrate active listening without actively engaging in critique yourself, for example, "I can understand that you are really upset that she has not come to take you for the weekend as she promised," or "I know that me moving further out of the city has made it harder for you to see your friends. What things could we think of together that would allow you to see them a bit more?" Allowing your child to express and communicate their feelings without judgment will help them to build trust with you and feel heard.

- Be Flexible:

Cancellations might happen for very valid reasons. Be willing to adapt where reasonable to accommodate your ex, and expect the same flexibility in return if something comes up at the last minute for you and you find yourself needing to cancel or make changes to spending time with your children.

- Do Not Argue in Front of Your Children:

Avoid arguing with your co-parent in front of your children. This will only cause stress and worry. Even if these discussions need to take place, keep them to phone calls, texts, or in the presence of a mediator.

- Practice Self-Care:

Whilst you might constantly be thinking of life post-divorce, or your child's well-being, make sure you keep up looking after yourself. This looks different for everybody but might include exercise, meditation, seeing friends, or other recreational hobbies.

Quick Review of Successful Co-Parenting

In summary, consider the following aspects when devising a co-parenting plan, supporting your children, and approaching your new relationship with your co-parent.

- Prioritize your children.
- Communication is key.
- Work together with your co-parent.
- Listen to your children and allow them to vent.
- Do not use your children as messengers.
- Keep a routine.
- Do not criticize your co-parent.
- Set goals and try to stick to them.
- In time, work on forgiving your co-parent.

Reflective Questions

1. *Your co-parent cancels their weekend plans for taking your child out to the movies last minute. They are distraught and keep saying that they feel unloved and that they are always being let down – how can you reassure them?*

2. *You have been pretty strict on getting your child to bed before 9 p.m. as agreed in your parenting plan, but they come back from a weekend with their other parent, and you hear how they stayed up until midnight every night. How do you best reach out to your co-parent and communicate that this could be an issue?*
3. *Your co-parent says that they want to take your child on a 3-week summer break with their new partner. You feel uncomfortable about this – what is the best approach to deal with this?*

Summary

In this chapter, we covered what co-parenting is, how to set up a clear and successful co-parenting plan, and how best to support your children in the transition into co-parenting.

Although all this information might seem daunting for now, you are on your way to being well-informed about how best to navigate the early stages of co-parenting. Should problems arise, you will know how to keep your calm and approach them, and you will be familiar with how best to support a child struggling with the effects of divorce.

In the next chapter, we will explore how to build a better parent-child relationship and reinforce how to best support your child and their well-being.

Chapter 3:
Building a Better Parent-Child Relationship

"The best inheritance a parent can give his children is a few minutes of his time each day."

— Orlando Aloysius Battista

My father had an affair. That is if you can call it that. It was not the case of a quick dalliance or a short fling with a colleague, but a relationship with a close family friend that lasted over four years. My mother later admitted that she knew early on, but decided to turn a blind eye to his late nights, poor excuses, and ill-thought-out lies. When my parents finally got divorced, I was livid. Seething, even. I wanted nothing to do with my father. In my eyes, he had betrayed my trust, abandoned our family, and forsaken my mother. It took years until we spoke again, and even now, I remain mistrustful; of both him and of relationships generally – although I do remain hopeful that if I can provide someone with the commitment and loyalty I know I am capable of, others out there can also do the same.

Repairing my relationship with my father was not an easy one. Yet, despite all the hurt he had caused her, my mother would encourage *me gently to respond to his attempts at reconciliation. I know that it pained her deeply, but still, she wanted me to grow up at least in contact with my father. He also persevered. Some letters and messages went unanswered, and gifts arrived like clockwork on my birthday. Our relationship is now far from perfect, but I am glad that he persisted, and that I found it within myself to forgive. I am glad that my mother finally found the courage to leave, and I am glad that my daughter gets to grow up with a granddad of her own – even if our family is made up of a patchwork of homes.*

The Importance of Parent-Child Relationship

Healthy parent-child relationships are incredibly important for building emotionally intelligent, confident, and well-rounded adults. Children who grow up with secure attachments to their parents tend to go on to have healthy and secure relationships with friends and partners in later life and tend also to perform better academically and socially. Equally, they have a better grasp of emotional regulation when it comes to stress and anger, and are less likely to suffer from mental health problems (Winston, Chicot, 2016).

The idea that how our relationships with our parents define how we present as adults is not a new concept. This focus on the importance of early nurturing has continued into the present day, with developmental psychologist Gordon Neufeld and physician Gabor Maté amongst those sharing quite how important positive physical early infant interactions and relationships are, and how they impact us later in life. "Children do not experience our intentions, no matter how heartfelt. They experience what we manifest in tone and behavior" (Maté, Neufeld, 2004).

Children thrive when they feel loved and supported. They form multiple attachments from infanthood onwards, all of which are incredibly important and beneficial to later developments in their character. The presence of both mother and father during this period enhances their ability to interact and learn from their parents and is therefore a key indicator of why it is important to try and find a suitable way for both parents to be involved post-divorce or separation, where possible.

Examples of Positive Parenting

Below are some behaviors and tactics you can implement that will help to reassure your children and foster a healthy parent-child relationship.

- Maintaining Boundaries:

Constructing clear boundaries provides children with structure and routine, under which they excel. This includes setting firm boundaries, as well as verbalizing expectations, and making sure that they understand the reasoning behind them. You can involve your children in constructing these rules to a degree, and provide incentives and rewards for good behavior; for example, telling them that they are expected to complete all their homework before the weekend, and in doing so, will be allowed to attend a party or event of their choosing at the weekend. For the younger children, eating all their despised vegetables might grant them access to a particularly cherished sweet treat or toy.

- Warmth, Empathy, and Reassurance:

Engaging positively through open and welcoming body language and eye contact reaffirms a loving relationship. This includes acknowledging feelings that your child experiences, and creating a safe space so that they may feel comfortable in coming to you to share any problems.

Examples of empathetic phrases include:

- "I understand that you feel that way."
- "I can see that you are having a really hard time right now."
- "I wish you did not have to go through all of this."
- "This must be a challenging time for you."
- "You are completely justified in feeling angry/sad/frustrated with us."
- "I am proud of you."
- "I will always be here for you, no matter what."
- "I am here if you want to talk about it, always."

Even if you do not agree with their feelings or responses, remaining supportive and always being ready to listen will encourage transparency in the relationship between you and your child both throughout their childhood and for their relationships in later life.

- Active Listening and Communication:

Active listening involves paying attention and demonstrating that you are listening through eye contact and encouraging gestures. It also requires no interruptions, and no jumping to conclusions or passing judgment. The listener should ask questions where necessary and provide feedback if deemed appropriate. Paraphrasing what has been said also demonstrates that the listener has been paying attention.

Active listening is a key part of parent-child relationships, and fine-tuning these skills will improve methods of communication, both between parent and child, and improve the children's listening skills for later life relationships.

- Problem-Solving:

Should a problem arise, rather than plowing ahead and solving it by yourself, allow for your child's input. Asking how they might solve the problem, providing feedback on their response, and then solving it together will help improve problem-solving skills. This varies between ages but can range from discussing how children fighting over one toy can agree, to playing chess with your teenagers and getting them to think two steps ahead.

How to Improve a Parent-Child Relationship

Alongside using the above techniques, consider how you can best show up for your child daily to reinforce your relationship with them.

- Be Present:

Put time aside each day to be available to your child when they are in your care, without any distractions from work or phone. Be readily available to listen to children when they have problems of their own, whether related to your divorce or their own life. When children feel like they can come to you at any point and you will be ready to listen, they will feel reassured and supported, and feelings of guilt or anxiety will often be reduced.

- Express Your Love and Reassurance:

Even during difficult periods or after arguing, a simple "I love you," goes a long way. Particularly for children who might feel like the rug has been swept out from under them post-divorce, and even if they struggle to communicate it in return, expressing affection verbally, through physical touch, or little gestures, will reassure them of your love.

- Listen and Communicate:

The active listening techniques mentioned earlier will help build a stronger connection between the parent and child. Where possible, keeping an open mind and trying to empathize with the child's perspective will also help build trust, even if you find yourself internally disagreeing with what they are saying. You might find yourself met with statements that even anger or upset you like:

"I feel like the divorce is all your fault, I wish you and Mom (or Dad) had stayed married and had not ruined my life".

Initially, you might be tempted to respond to a statement like the above with anger, or begin criticizing your ex to your child and letting them know what a piece of work their other parent is. However, finding methods to calm and compose yourself, taking a big breath, and then responding with a statement that shows you empathize and are willing to listen and work through their concerns will often get you further in building trust and fostering a connection in the long run.

For example, "I can see that you are upset about this all. I am sorry that you have had to go through so many changes in the past six months. I know that you wish your mother (or father) and I had stayed married, but unfortunately, that was not possible anymore. I am glad you have shared your feelings with me, and I hope we can talk about some ways to help make you feel better about the current situation."

- Eat Meals Together:

Between work and school, family members often miss spending quality time together as everyone is incredibly busy. This can contribute to feelings of loneliness or resentment after a divorce when it is critical that children feel heard and supported. Where possible, taking time to start or finish off the day with a meal together keeps all family members on the same page, and can contribute to bonding as a family. This often means turning off phones and the television, so you can all fully focus on engaging with one another without distractions.

- Spend Quality Time Together:

Whether it is going to the movies, on holiday, to a football game, or spending a few hours playing with toys – children will appreciate you giving them your full attention, reassuring them, particularly during stressful periods like divorce, that they remain a priority. Developing regular routines and traditions can help foster a feeling of consistent and enjoyable routine; for example, reading them a bedtime story every night, or going out for dinner every Friday.

- Plan Ahead:

As you set out your co-parenting plan, you will have realized how much planning and organization go into parenting after a divorce. The efforts needed to coordinate holidays, drop-offs, big decisions, and everything in between are also crucial for keeping in touch with your children. Making sure to organize and allocate regular time to spend together will help your children feel like they are still a key focus in your life. This can mean attending sporting events, going to watch their favorite movies, or taking them out for their favorite meals. Keeping your children in the loop as to when they will be spending time with you will help you bond together and create new fun memories post-divorce.

- Make the Most of Your Time Together:

Even if you are having a bad day, whether it is work, life, or your struggles with navigating life after a divorce, try to put those feelings away in the time you set aside for your children. This means putting your phone down and tuning out from the outside world so that your children feel appreciated and you can make the most of your time together.

- Try New Hobbies:

The hobbies do not have to be new, but finding a shared interest can lead to long-term benefits and enjoyment. If your child is interested in gaming, try and keep up to date with their favorite games and play together. If they like tennis, incorporate it into your schedule when possible. If they like art and painting, suggest drawing together. Alternatively, try reading their favorite books so that you can discuss them. Learning what your child likes and showing active interest in their hobbies will foster a positive connection, and give you something mutual to continue enjoying together.

- Use Technology:

The world is filled with new methods of communication. Facetiming and texting regularly can help you to stay in contact with your kids – even if they are spending time with their co-parent. Be cautious not to seem overbearing in the time you spend apart, and avoid texting them incessantly when they are in the care of their other parent, but use technology to your advantage to maintain your relationship.

- Stay Positive:

As tempting as criticizing your ex might be in the presence of your child, avoid doing so. Verbal accusations or denigration will lead to resentment and feelings of hurt – either toward you or their co-parent – and can lead to potential loyal conflicts or other negative consequences. Demonstrating quiet respect from afar will benefit healing on all sides.

- Where Possible, Live Close to Your Co-Parent:

If you choose shared custody, moving between two homes will often be stressful enough at the start. This is made even more stressful if the two residences are far apart, and involve huge commute times. Living close by, when possible, will reduce anxiety from traveling and will mean that important factors such as school and friends can stay as they are. Small crises, like leaving their favorite toy at their other parent's house, can also be quickly remedied by a short drive.

- Be Considerate When Introducing New Partners:

It is almost inevitable that one or both parents will find a new romantic partner at some point after separation. This can be a pretty big hurdle for children to face. It is the conclusion of "Mom and Dad are not getting back together," which can be incredibly difficult for them to come to terms with. Additionally, your children might feel guilty about allowing a new stepparent into their lives out of loyalty to their biological mom or dad.

How these new partners are introduced to your children, and how much involvement they should have in the lives of your children, is something that should be set out and agreed upon in the co-parenting plan. Nonetheless, the initial introduction of a new partner can be anxiety-inducing for everyone involved. Be mindful of how you date, how much you share with your children, how and when you introduce your partners to your children, and how you speak about your ex doing so themselves.

Changes in Your Relationship After Divorce

It is very normal to experience changes in your relationship with your child post-divorce. Owing to the huge number of changes going on in the child's life, it would be unusual for them not to show some level of behavior change. This is most obvious in children experiencing high-conflict divorces, and can display as one or more of the following:

- Withdrawal:

Children may withdraw from their relationship with their parents, and be unwilling to communicate or express how they are feeling. This is particularly prevalent in divorces where one parent holds primary custody, and the other parent sees the child less, or where there is a conflict of loyalty where the child places more blame on one parent for instigating the separation.

- Lack of Respect and Hostility:

Particularly in cases of high-conflict divorce, children may come to resent one or both parents for the breakup and the upheaval of their lives. They may channel this anger into hostility, by talking back, acting out, and pushing boundaries. This lack of respect will also likely be directed at their parents' future new partners.

Why Your Child Might Be Feeling Angry and Why They Are Taking it out on You

It is not uncommon that a child blames one parent over the other for causing the divorce, and side with the parent that they feel was wronged in the process. Feeling like your child hates you also piles on a mountain of extra emotions that make dealing with divorce and separation even more burdensome. You or your ex might unknowingly reinforce these feelings in your child by talking negatively about each other, which although tempting, is best avoided as can affect the relationships your children have with their parents in the long term. More on this can be found in Chapter 6.

Signs that your child is blaming you might include:

- Verbalizing anger and hate
- Withdrawing and refusing to engage in conversation
- Refusing to spend time with you
- Siding with their other parent

Working With Your Ex

It can be incredibly difficult to try and put your differences aside and cooperate with your ex in taking action against a frustrated and resentful child. However, as children benefit most from positive relations with both parents, putting your own emotions on the back burner and prioritizing your child will be most beneficial in helping your child navigate life post-divorce.

- Be sure to communicate any concerns with your co-parent, particularly when it comes to worries about new behaviors your child might be exhibiting, and come to a mutual understanding of how you will both respond.

- Remain civil. It might be tempting to blame your co-parent for your child's sudden anger but try to demonstrate that even post-divorce or separation, you can maintain a united front and work together.

- Keep your focus on your child, not on yourself. You might want to vent about feeling scorned and left out, particularly if you feel like you are the parent bearing the brunt of rejection. However, try to keep the focus and your priority on your children, and how to move forward with their best interests at heart, instead of venting about how the situation is making you feel. Continue to express your own emotions, but do so in the presence of your family members and close circle.

When Your Ex Will Not Cooperate

Not all parents are capable of putting their own emotions aside and focusing on the well-being of their children. If you find yourself met with a co-parent who proves difficult to work alongside, who might even be acting out of spite and targeting you, it is worth seeking outside support through counseling or court involvement. Also consider alternative parenting measures, like parallel parenting – explored in Chapter 5.

What to Do if You Feel Like Your Child Hates You

- Communicate:

Communication can be incredibly difficult if it is one-sided. However, remain persistent. Even if your child seems unwilling to engage, do not give up. Commitment and perseverance will demonstrate love and stability to your child; particularly at a time when children will feel vulnerable and unstable in their relationships with both parents. Do not take silence or a lack of reciprocation to heart. Repairing and building new relationships with your children after divorce takes time.

- Do Not Take Your Child's Emotions Personally:

Hearing "I hate you," from your child can be like a dagger to the heart. However, remember that divorce and separation intensify the emotions that everyone is feeling. Try not to take these outbursts personally, and work to find methods to calm your own emotions and respond in a composed manner.

- Set Boundaries:

Whilst you should be encouraging your children to express their emotions, be consistent in boundary setting and do not allow excessive disrespect of you or your co-parent. For children who demand that they want to spend time with one parent and one parent alone, work with your co-parent on finding the best solution for your situation – whether this means allocated time with each parent even if they insist against it, or a period apart.

- Remember That You Want Your Children to Appreciate Their Other Parent:

It is okay to feel left out, and at times jealous. Having a child that is withdrawing from you, slamming doors, refusing to talk to you, and demanding that they spend all their time with their other parent can be difficult to process. However, try to remember that children benefit most from strong relationships with *both* parents. You want your child to love their other parent. Continue to show up for them, demonstrate your love and commitment, and in time, when their emotions are less amplified, your children will likely fall into a more harmonized relationship with both parents.

- Respect Your Children:

This largely applies to teenagers and children old enough to make their own decisions. Avoid patronizing them and talking down to them, as this will likely only enflame their anger further. Engage with them appropriately, and listen to their emotions and concerns without voicing judgment or meeting them with anger, which will encourage a relationship of transparency and trust.

- Consider Therapy or Counseling:

Sometimes, managing your own emotions or those of your children can be simply too much to bear on your own. Consider family or individual counseling where possible, as involvement from an outside party can help mediate and introduce methods to reduce conflict and restore trust in relationships.

- Take a Step Back:

If you are trying your best, and still finding yourself constantly up against a hard wall when it comes to engaging with your child, it is okay to take a step back for a while. Persistence and perseverance are key, but there may come a time when it is in your and your child's best interest to take a step back and let them go. Acknowledge their anger and resentment if they blame you, give them space, and respect their decision. Remind them that you will always be here should they need support, but allow them the time to grieve their previous family life.

Child Discipline

If you do find yourself with a child who is acting out beyond their usual self, questioning authority, and defying boundaries, the first step is setting clear discipline expectations with your co-parent, to make sure you are both on the same page. Approaches will vary in every parent-child relationship, and the outcomes encourage not just safer behavior, but also help children to develop into responsible adults.

Setting boundaries and consequences for failing to follow them tends to help children feel less anxious, as they benefit from guidance and leadership from their parents.

Setting appropriate expectations and boundaries also encourages children to make good choices and benefits their problem-solving skills. You will no doubt have some push-back – particularly from teenagers – but educating your children about the risks of dangerous behaviors like substance abuse or drunk driving, and providing adequate discipline should they still choose to engage, will encourage them to make well-thought decisions in the future.

Discipline need also not be negative. Positive discipline can involve using praise and rewards to acknowledge positive behavior and reinforce good choices, which will often reduce their temptation to engage poorly later on.

Discipline is not to be confused with punishment; particularly physical punishment. Physical punishment has been linked to a myriad of issues including negative self-esteem, potential injuries, impaired views of justice, and above all, damage to the parent-child relationship.

Instead, set age-appropriate punishments. This can be decided between you and your co-parent and can range from time out for small children, to confiscation of phones or limited gaming for older children. Avoid being irrational with these disciplinary measures – "That is it, I am taking your phone away forever," will likely be met with more resistance and resentment than a reasonable consequence.

Deciding on Discipline in Co-Parenting Situations

It can be difficult to find a middle ground in how to approach discipline with a co-parent.

- Agree on Disciplinary Expectations With Your Ex:

You and your ex might not see eye to eye when it comes to how to discipline your children, and what even counts as misbehaving. These are all elements that should be covered in your co-parenting plan. Maintain a degree of flexibility and be willing to listen and negotiate over what you consider fair with your ex, and try to come to as much an agreement as possible as to what is and is not allowed, and how to deal with children breaching these boundaries.

- Be Consistent With Your Boundaries and Discipline:

If your child gets to stay up late at one parent's house or watch shows one parent deems inappropriate and then gets scolded by the other parent, this will undoubtedly lead to some degree of resentment. Mistakes happen, but try to maintain consistency in setting rules and sticking to them. This also counts for discipline and consequences; one parent responding to rule-breaking by removing their child's phone for a week, and the other only giving a dismissive telling-off will also contribute to feelings of resentment towards the stricter parent. Try to stay on the same page as your ex and approach discipline as a team.

- Communicate With Your Children:

Be sure to communicate the rules you have set out with your ex to your children, so they too are aware of what they are and are not allowed to do, and the consequences that might follow if they were to break these rules. Listen to your children's input when it comes to how they feel about certain rules, even if you are unwilling to bend on these fronts and allow a certain degree of flexibility over certain boundaries; for example, letting them stay up longer on weekends if they prove to behave exceptionally well during the week. Good behavior can also be rewarded not only by positive verbal praise but also by positive reinforcements such as greater leniency and treats.

- Try to Determine Why Your Children Are Misbehaving:

If you do notice your children acting out far more than usual, try to determine why. They might be hesitant in opening up, but demonstrate that you are eager and willing to listen to their perspective, which will encourage them to share their feeling and often uncover the source of anger or trauma which is causing flare-ups.

- Avoid Villainizing Your Ex:

Your co-parent might feel strongly about certain rules which you are less concerned with, or vice versa. Approach setting up discipline expectations with flexibility, and avoid trying to win over your children by allowing them more leniency on these rules.

- Do Not Get Guilt-Tripped Into Leniency:

Following on from the above, whilst you should ideally maintain the rules that your ex insists on, that is not to say that your ex will do the same for the rules you care strongly for. In these cases, you might be met with "Well, Dad lets me do this!" In these situations, it might be tempting to bend and fold, however, remind your child that the rules in your house are different. Communicate these issues with your co-parent when appropriate to try and maintain as much consistency where possible, but also be sure to uphold your expectations, rules, and consequences for breaking them.

Quick Tips for Effective Discipline in a Co-Parenting Situation

In review, these are the points to consider when considering how to approach effective and consistent discipline.

- Keep your children busy.
- Use positive reinforcement.
- Keep calm and composed, even if you are feeling angry.
- Stick to consistent and clear boundaries which you have

decided upon with your co-parent.
- Communicate with your children and involve them in boundary-setting.

Common Mistakes in Discipline With a Co-Parent

Avoid also falling into the pitfalls of any of the following when considering how you enforce discipline with your children.

- Working *against* your co-parent, not with them
- Being inconsistent in rules, expectations, and consequences
- Trying to win your child over by being the more lenient parent
- Creating overly strict rules or harsh consequences for misbehavior
- Using your child to relay messages to your ex instead of communicating with them directly

Reflective Questions

1. You feel strongly about not allowing your child to go to a high school party, but your ex says that they think your child should be allowed to go. Despite putting your foot down, your child attends the party whilst spending the weekend with your co-parent. How do you respond to both your child and your co-parent?

2. What are some positive reinforcements that apply to your child, that you know that they will respond to and that you could use to encourage good behavior?

3. *What are some negative consequences that apply to your child, that you might suggest to your co-parent and that you can both use should your child act out?*

Summary

In this chapter, we covered how parent-child relationships might be negatively impacted post-divorce, and how to improve your relationship with your child should problems arise. We have also explored how to implement a useful approach to consistent discipline with your co-parent, and what to do if you feel like your child is taking out their anger toward the divorce on you or your co-parent.

In the next chapter, you will learn more about what to do when your co-parent is uncooperative and unwilling to work cohesively with you on implementing important boundaries and expectations.

Chapter 4:
The Toxic Co-Parent

"The more dysfunctional, the more family members seek to control the behavior of others."
– David W. Earle

I did not exactly have to work hard to conclude that my ex was toxic. He was toxic both in our marriage and in how he attempted to parent after we separated. The unfortunate thing is that some people are pretty good at acting. They can play out the role of being kind and selfless and generous. I fell head over heels for the man who bought me flowers and surprised me with little thoughtful gifts and mopped my fevered brow when I got sick. The warning signs were few and far between, and easy to overlook when everything else seemed to be going so well. The thing with toxic people is that also, unfortunately, they cannot keep up their role forever. The rose-tinted glass fell away, and he started to become more and more controlling. I was not to see my closest friends anymore – they did not have my best interests at heart. Did I have to go to the gym? Couldn't I spend more time at home? Why did I get home so late after a night out? Be home by midnight. Then 11 p.m. Better yet, stop going out at all. My clothes were too drab or my skirts too short, and my makeup was either too thick or not enough.

He was also a master manipulator, and I found myself starting to doubt even my thoughts, let alone those of my friends and family.

These traits carried on into our divorce. Although we were both so deeply unhappy in our marriage, he seemed even unhappier and angry even, at the prospect of having to separate. We could not be happy together but I certainly was not allowed to be happy apart either. At no point did he stop and think about the effect this was having on our daughter. I was barraged by angry messages and calls, and any in-person contact would often lead to him shouting about how bad a mother I was. On the weeks that he did care for our daughter, she would often come back to my home sullen and red-eyed. It took a lot of coaxing, but she would often eventually open up and tell me that he had spent their time together berating her, saying she was not good enough at school, and making her feel guilty for the time that she spent with me.

This left me distraught. Our daughter was having a hard enough time coming to terms with having to move between one house and the other, alongside all the new changes in her life. Surely, we should be working together to help her through it, not making it harder for her.

Unfortunately, the reality is that not every parent is capable or willing to put the needs of their children above their own, least of all toxic parents.

Signs You Are Dealing With a Toxic Co-Parent

Co-parenting works best when both parents prioritize the well-being of their children above everything else. Toxic co-parents tend to do the opposite; they put themselves above their children, push boundaries, and will often attack their ex's character even when unprovoked. Many toxic co-parents can even be defined as having narcissistic personality tendencies, which tend to signify having exaggerated self-worth, a lack of empathy, and a lack of compassion for others.

There is a line between an uncooperative co-parent and a toxic one. Life after a divorce is not easy, especially when you have to stay in contact with someone whom you shared a large part of your life with, and probably had or still have strong feelings for. Even non-toxic individuals might be difficult to deal with on some days. However, individuals that constantly exhibit one or more of the signs below can be classified as toxic co-parents. They will no doubt make co-parenting a lot more difficult, and it is worth keeping an eye on their behavior to see if and how your parenting plan needs to be adjusted in response to negative conduct.

- Disagreeing to Even Reasonable Divorce and Custodial Arrangements:

Disagreeing over certain rules or expectations, bedtimes, what your child should eat, what they can watch – it is all quite normal. You will tend to come to some form of agreement or leniency at some point down the line in a more normal co-parenting situation, even if it takes a little trial and error.

A toxic co-parent will however fight you every step of the way. Even small issues will be blown out of proportion, and you will often find them arguing counterintuitively over what is best for your child, just so that they get their chance to rile you up and cause some form of conflict. Even if you come to agreements over certain rules and expectations, toxic co-parents will often fail to follow them in practice.

- Manipulating You or Your Children, Often Weaponizing Them and Turning Them Against You:

Children will already be feeling a lot of emotions after a divorce. Most parents will work to soothe and reassure them as much as possible. Toxic parents will however see this as an opportunity to alienate them from you, by talking badly about you to your children and trying to attack your character.

Children thrive best when they have the loving support of both parents, but toxic parents care little for this fact. They will manipulate them and use their vulnerability to try and turn them against you.

- May Play 'Hot and Cold', by Claiming to Miss You and Trying to Win You Back, Then Reverting to Acting With Hostility:

Toxic individuals will often struggle with letting go of you and your marriage and may be unable to work on healing themselves or allowing you to heal. They might try and claim one minute that they miss you and want you back, or stonewall and ignore you completely the next, even when your parenting plan requires some degree of communication. Toxic and narcissistic individuals will often go from one extreme emotion to the other, making it very difficult for people in their presence to relax as they often remain on edge about what might set the toxic individual off, and whether they are currently in a good or bad mood.

- Punishing Your Children for Your Behavior:

A toxic parent who still feels sharply about a divorce or separation might try and take these feelings of anger out on their children. They might punish them, rescind their affection, or work otherwise to try and hurt you by hurting your children.

- Refusing to Be Flexible to the Needs of You or Your Children:

As with disagreeing over anything, toxic co-parents will be unwilling to cater to any cancellations. They will show no flexibility or understanding of changing plans, or respect for your life and other responsibilities you might have. On the whole, they will be very uncooperative and difficult to work with.

- Inflated Ego and Arrogant Personality:

Toxic and narcissistic individuals in particular think incredibly highly of themselves. They are often hugely arrogant and proud and demand the praise of others. They can take no criticism and think of themselves as often perfect and unparalleled. This might filter through to your children in unhelpful and toxic statements such as, "Well, you love me more than Mom (or Dad), right?"

- Inability to Express or Demonstrate Empathy to You or Your Children:

Whilst toxic individuals require a large amount of praise and adoration, they often do not grant others the same. They lack empathy and understanding and are callous and uncaring when it comes to understanding the needs of others. They also lack emotional intelligence, and will often not provide your children with empathetic love and support.

There will also be no wishing you well and letting you move on with your life. Toxic exes will often demand knowing about your new partners, which will send them spiraling into rage or attempts to control or hurt you or your children.

- Extreme Feelings of Jealousy:

Toxic individuals, although viewing themselves as god-like, are often still inherently jealous and spiteful. They might be jealous of you, for moving on with your life, or even absurdly jealous of your children. This behavior might manifest in negative comments about appearance or intelligence if they seek to bring others down out of jealousy. They will often have no filter when it comes to criticizing your child on difficult topics, be it about weight or academic performance.

How a Toxic Parent Raises Their Children

Toxic parents can unfortunately have a long-lasting impact on their children, as their parenting tends to be very selfish and emotionally reactive.

- Seeing Their Children as Commodities:

It is normal to be proud of your children when they do well at school, win at a sporting event, or take home the title of a spelling bee. Toxic co-parents will take this a step further. They see their children as an item of value or a commodity. They brag and boast about them beyond the normal amount, and stretch to do so for things like physical appearance or intelligence. They will appear competitive and pit their children against others, and will often be enraged and unsympathetic to any losses.

- Emotionally Reactive and Hostile:

Equally, when their child does not perform well or fails to please, or even upsets them in a certain way – even if unintentionally so – a toxic or narcissistic parent will react with sudden outbursts of anger and aggression. They will lash out, whether in screaming fits, or even physical aggression. They may also gaslight their child by turning around situations to unfairly blame them, making them feel as if even the parent's hostility is the fault of the child – which leads to issues such as anxiety and hypervigilance in later life.

- Selfishness:

Toxic parents will struggle to do the one thing that is most important in navigating life post-divorce; they will almost inevitably fail to put their children's needs first. Of course, this is not always possible in life. Sometimes, parents will have to put the needs of their children behind their own, and miss out on a promised game night if they have a late-night shift, or ask them to help out with extra chores if they are overwhelmed with housework alongside earning money. However, toxic parents will always put themselves above everyone else. They will insist that their children stay up to babysit their siblings so that they can go out clubbing, or force them to sacrifice their hobbies to partake in the interests of the parent.

- Lacking Empathy:

Toxic parents know no sympathy or empathy. Attempting to explain your feelings to them will often be fruitless. They fail to comprehend the consequences of their actions and how they impact others and will show little to no understanding of the emotions of others. Children will often be wary of sharing their feelings with toxic parents out of fear of how they might respond, leading to adults who have difficulty opening up.

- Poor Boundaries:

Whilst we have emphasized the importance of boundaries in co-parenting relationships, it is unfortunate that toxic co-parents struggle with boundaries, and have next to none. They might be intrusive and overly involved in the lives of their children; maybe tracking their every step, limiting them from doing even suitable age-appropriate activities, logging on to their social media without prior consent, and restricting every element of their child's lives. Equally, they might be overly critical of their child, and go as far as to comment on their appearance, weight, or intellect, thus constantly bringing them down without awareness or care for the impact this has upon their children's confidence and self-worth.

- Expecting to Be Cared For:

In a reversal of roles, toxic parents will often expect their children to care for them. They will expect their children to take up most of the household duties and do tasks such as cooking and cleaning for the parent. They might claim that their child owes them for raising them and housing them, and thus they are indebted to their toxic parent and must go above and beyond to grant all of their wishes and make this parent the center of their universe.

How Toxic Parents Affect Children's Mental Health

Being raised by someone who pits you against yourself and never shows any compassion or care can have long-lasting effects on children, and leave them with numerous behavioral issues.

- Negative Self-Worth:

Constant gaslighting and criticizing will often leave a child with their confidence in tatters. They will struggle to see themselves as a worthwhile individual and will be unable to find any redeemable qualities in themselves. This will often leave an adult with very low self-worth, who feels like they have nothing to offer the world, or other mental health problems such as anxiety or depression.

- Overly Selfless:

Being aware and conscious of other individuals is a wonderful trait. However, children of toxic parents will go above and beyond this and often be unable to gauge nor satisfy their own needs. They will be so used to catering to their parent above everyone else that they will struggle to care for themselves, and often feel extreme guilt when trying to determine how to incorporate future friends or partners into their life, and how to prioritize the needs of these future individuals. They might appear incredibly selfless and kind, but putting everyone else above themselves will make them easy targets for other narcissistic individuals to take advantage of.

- Insecure Attachment Style:

Children of toxic parents will be strangers to feeling reassured, loved, and comforted. The constant highs and lows of their childhood relationship with this parent will contribute to feelings of mistrust toward other individuals in later life. They might appear overly independent, as they will have never felt that they had anyone to rely on growing up. Equally, they might appear overly needy and clingy toward their partner, requiring constant affection and reassurance to feel even slightly comforted, and even then, push their partners away out of self-sabotage and feeling undeserving of love.

- Anxiety and Hypervigilance:

An unpredictable parent leads to an anxious child. This might manifest in mental health problems such as obsessive-compulsive disorder (OCD) or other manifestations of anxiety. This will often lead to a child who is always on high alert and in fight or flight mode, having always had to monitor their parent for signs of mood changes or outbursts.

- Guilt and Self-Blame:

A toxic parent will often blame a child for their emotional outbursts or issues in life. This blame will filter on into later life, with these individuals often quick to feel themselves at fault for situations in which they are not even remotely responsible.

- Repeat Cycle:

Unfortunately, children of narcissistic and toxic co-parents are often those who will later fall prey to relationships with people who also suffer from similar tendencies. They might find comfort in the gaslighting, criticizing, and extreme highs and lows of such a relationship. They will also rarely fight back against any denunciations of their character, and their self-worth will continue to spiral whilst in an active relationship with a toxic individual or narcissist.

Dealing With a Toxic Co-Parent

Co-parenting is tricky enough as is. It is made even harder by someone who is often emotionally manipulative, selfish, and willing to alienate your children against you whilst making life post-divorce a war instead of a collaboration. Whilst the next chapter explores parallel parenting, which is often a better choice for those attempting to co-parent with an incredibly toxic or difficult ex, it is worth still giving co-parenting a shot even with a difficult ex before you completely separate your lives.

- Set Out Your Own Goals and Stick to Them:

Sit down and set out what you envision as your parenting goals and values. How do you want to raise your children? What do you consider appropriate when it comes to big topics such as schooling, religion, screen time, or discipline? Where possible, sit down with your co-parent and discuss these goals. However, if you find yourself disagreeing on all your expectations, it might be worth moving to parallel parenting – where you raise your children in separate households with different expectations – to avoid conflict and disagreements with a co-parent who is unwilling to meet you halfway on anything.

- Create Your Household:

Make your home a safe space for your children, and focus your energy on them when you have time together. Avoid asking questions about what your ex is up to, if they are seeing a new partner, or how they are parenting your children. Instead, try and work on your parent-child relationship to the best of your abilities whilst with your children. Enjoy your time together, and work on building your new life.

- Allow Your Children to Have Their Relationship With Their Other Parent:

Despite any feelings of anger or resentment you might be harboring, allow your children to have a guilt-free relationship with their other parent. Children benefit most from healthy relationships with both parents and criticizing your ex or badmouthing them in front of your children might lead to parental alienation. Only in situations where a parent is completely unfit to parent out of anger or behavioral issues, substance abuse, or if they pose an actual threat to the well-being of your children, should you move to seek full custody and parent alone.

- Avoid Triggering Your Ex or Responding to Being Baited:

Having been in some form of a romantic relationship for some time before your divorce or separation, you no doubt know your ex better than most people. You will know their likes and dislikes, and what upsets them. Although it might be tempting to use this to your advantage in defaming their character, and in a personal vendetta of your hurt after separation, use your knowledge of their triggers to your advantage and avoid them where possible.

Equally, know whilst you might be attempting to be the bigger person and do so yourself, your ex might use their knowledge of your personality and your triggers to their advantage. Where possible, find ways to keep yourself calm and composed and avoid rising to be taunted or baited.

- Maintain Firm Boundaries:

Setting out clear and firm boundaries for what is and is not acceptable will lead to less conflict of one co-parent upsetting the other. Toxic parents will often try to test these boundaries, even purposefully seeking them out and pushing you to your limit. Maintain your own set of rules and expectations and stand your ground. If you find yourself repeatedly being taken advantage of, seek support from a third-party mediator, or even court, to try and encourage your co-parent to respect and adhere to your boundaries.

Sticking to Your Boundaries

Talking about sticking to your boundaries and being strong is one thing – doing so, particularly after an emotionally heavy and tiresome divorce is quite another. However, learning how to do so and implementing those techniques is particularly important when dealing with a toxic and uncooperative co-parent.

- Stick to Your Parenting Plan:

As explored in the previous chapter, a set-out, and detailed parenting plan is key to successful co-parenting. A toxic or narcissistic co-parent might well try and push the boundaries you set out in the plan, or fail to adhere to the rules and expectations you set out together. Be aware of this, but try where possible to stick to the plan yourself.

- Keep Communication to a Minimum:

Whilst you might have set out expected communication standards, a toxic co-parent might ignore your requests. Do not rise to the bait of unwanted late-night texts and calls. Ignore any unnecessary communication, and politely remind your co-parent of what communication standards you set out in your co-parenting plan.

- Keep Calm and Composed:

You might find yourself triggered or baited by a toxic co-parent; particularly one who knows your weak spots. Exploring methods that you can use to take a step back from any situation where you feel yourself being riled up will help to avoid flare-ups. Toxic parents and narcissists are often looking for a reaction, and by ignoring them or failing to rise to their baits, you are doing yourself a favor and also not giving them the satisfaction of seeing you challenged by their behavior. Techniques you can use to calm yourself will vary but can include mindfulness and meditation, taking a short walk when you feel yourself particularly enraged, or calling a close friend.

- Refrain From Involving Your Children:

It might be tempting to vent to your children about a particularly toxic co-parent. Your children might also be unaware of quite how difficult your co-parent is making your life. They might see them in a completely different light, especially if your co-parent is doing well to manipulate your children and win them over. However, refrain from involving your children in your emotional turmoil. Do not use them to send messages to your ex, and if they start relaying messages from your ex, tell them politely that this is not something they need to be concerned about or involved with. Remind your co-parent that involving your children in your issues is unacceptable.

- Look Out for Manipulative or Controlling Behavior:

You might find that a toxic co-parent is unable to give you the satisfaction of moving on with your life. They might try to weaponize your children against you, or give you consequences for what they deem to be bad parenting on your part; for instance, not sticking to your custody schedule, not letting you see your children in your allocated periods, or dropping them off with you last minute. Be wary of any emotional manipulation and gaslighting, and if needed, escalate the behavior to court.

- Record Everything:

If you do find yourself back in court, or having to involve some alternative third-party mediation, you will be thankful you started recording every interaction you had with your ex. Particularly if those interactions were emotionally volatile and reactive, and you found yourself on the tail end of abuse. Keep track of text messages, calls, and in-person interactions by calendars or journals. This will firstly help organize your life, but also prove incredibly useful should you ever need to prove how destructive your co-parent was being.

- Involve a Mediator:

For a toxic co-parent who is failing to cooperate with you, you might find you need to involve a third party to remind them of their duties as a parent and caregiver to your child. This might be an escalation to court, to someone you both know and trust or to a family therapist. Whilst a toxic co-parent might not respect you, hearing firm words from an additional party might do well to remind them of their role, and encourage them to step back from antagonizing you and instead focus on parenting.

- Ditch Co-Parenting and Move to Parallel Parenting:

If your co-parenting attempts fail, it is not the end of the world. Many parents struggle with communicating regularly with a person with whom they were so intrinsically linked, and at one point romantically involved with. Toxic co-parents, in particular, will often be unable to regularly engage with a co-parent, and will instead appear as if on some personal vendetta against their ex, rather than prioritizing their children. Parallel parenting involves cutting off all communication and parenting separately – and is often the best solution for parenting with a toxic individual who is unable to move on from the past, and focuses instead on actively hurting you emotionally.

Empowering Others in the Co-Parenting Journey

"Courage is not the absence of fear, but the triumph over it."

- Nelson Mandela

For many individuals who find themselves in the challenging situation of co-parenting with a toxic ex, discovering resources like this book can be a lifeline. Finally, there is a sense of understanding, validation, and guidance on how to navigate the complexities of this difficult journey.

Before finding this book, you may have felt isolated and overwhelmed, uncertain of how to move forward while prioritizing the well-being of your children. The truth is, you are not alone, and countless others face similar challenges in their co-parenting experience.

The purpose of this book is not only to provide you with tips and strategies to overcome these obstacles but also to remind you that there is a community of individuals who share your struggles. And you can help spread this message of hope and empowerment to others in need. The best part? It only takes a few minutes of your time.

By sharing your genuine and honest opinion of this book on Amazon, you will show prospective readers that they are part of a larger community of individuals navigating the challenges of co-parenting with a difficult ex-partner. Your review will also direct them to a valuable resource that can truly make a difference in their lives.

Simply share how this book has helped you and what others can expect to find within its pages. By doing so, you will reassure other readers that they are not alone in their struggles and that there is support available to help them manage the complexities of co-parenting with a toxic ex.

Not only that, but your review will also guide them to the help they need with just a few clicks of a button.

Please know that I value all feedback, be it positive or negative, and I am eager to learn from your thoughts and experiences.

Thank you for your time, and I look forward to reading your review. Together, we can create a positive change in the lives of those navigating the challenges of co-parenting with a toxic ex, providing them with the tools, hope, and reassurance they need to persevere.

Scan to leave a review

Reflective Questions

1. You get a late-night text from your co-parent, shaming you for being a bad parent and calling you a bad person. How do you respond? Do you respond at all?
2. Your child gets home from a weekend at their other parent's house in floods of tears. You hear that your co-parent has made negative comments about their appearance, and left them distraught. What do you do?
3. Your children tell you that their other parent has spent the weekend badmouthing you to them. What is the best approach for responding to your children, and then speaking with your co-parent about this behavior?

Summary

In this chapter, we have covered how to spot a toxic co-parent, and how their selfish and manipulative behavior can impact their children, leaving them with life-long consequences such as damaged self-esteem and anxiety. We have also explored how to approach co-parenting with a toxic co-parent, and how to reaffirm your boundaries to try to do so successfully.

In the next chapter, we will explore parallel parenting, which is often the best solution for parents struggling with the communication and involvement of co-parenting, and for those who are unable to parent alongside a particularly toxic co-parent.

Chapter 5:
Parallel Parenting

"Leave your pride, ego, and narcissism somewhere else. Reactions from those parts of you will reinforce your children's most primitive fears."

— Henry Cloud

*A*fter we first split, I think I was naive in thinking that co-parenting would be easy. After all, we had been together for eight years. Even if the last few years of our marriage had been dreadful, and our little girl had fallen onto the back burner of our priorities, I was hopeful that in separation, we would be able to work together to make her our number one concern.

We were not on the best of terms, but he said he would chip in for the school run. We agreed that she would be in bed by 9 p.m. on school nights, and always needed a generous serving of greens at dinner. Gradually, however, the texts got a little more caustic. He was busy, he could not pick her up. Why couldn't I do it? Why was I being so lazy?

When he did take her for a weekend, he would drop her off late on Sunday evening with dark circles around her eyes, after which she would spend most of the night glowering wide-eyed and insisting on *more hours of television. I would be on my phone in a frenzy, sending angry text messages about how he was failing to comply with the schedule we had set out together. The next time he came to pick her up, we would be knee-deep in a shouting match before our daughter had even left the house. Co-parenting was not working for us.*

What Is Parallel Parenting?

For those who do not slot into the ease of co-parenting, and particularly those who do not end things on the best of terms, parallel parenting comes into play.

I know that amicable divorces happen. I have had friends run me through the cheeriness of spending Christmas and birthdays with their divorced and present partners, sharing gifts and toasts, and playing big happy families.

For those who are not quite as lucky, parallel parenting means removing that involvement. It means both parents disengaging from each other, to minimize communication and reduce conflict to as little as possible. It is usually the solution for high-conflict divorces or separations and tends to be the best solution for parents who struggle to get along amongst themselves but still need to show up for their children. It can also be temporary, for those who want to work toward a more aligned goal of communicative co-parenting.

Co-Parenting Versus Parallel Parenting

As explained in earlier chapters, co-parenting involves a great deal more alignment of values. Co-parenting generally works well for parents who can engage regularly through all forms of communication, including face-to-face meetings, and can agree on cohesive and consistent approaches to how they want to raise their children. By contrast, parallel parenting removes this element of regular communication for parents who struggle to maintain regular communication without instigating conflict and allows each parent to approach their parenting styles separately.

How Does Successful Parallel Parenting Benefit Children?

Similar to successful co-parenting, successful parallel parenting benefits children immensely and provides them with a strong foundation after a divorce or separation, leading to:

- Fewer behavior problems
- Fewer emotional problems
- Higher self-esteem
- Better school performance
- Better family relationships

Benefits of Parallel Parenting

Parallel parenting is also hugely beneficial to parents as well as children, as it can minimize conflict and allow high-conflict co-parents to get along from a distance.

- Reduced Interaction:

Since any form of interaction between estranged parents tends to result in conflict (think name-calling, accusations, resentment, or just plainly being ignored), parallel parenting means minimizing any form of interaction which could lead to all of the above. That means eliminating any avoidable conversations such as phone calls and texts and finding alternative ways to communicate and organize necessities such as planning appointments and outlining schedules. Using an assigned mediator or parenting coordinator can often help organize effective communication between parents.

- Reduced Stress and Conflict:

By removing unnecessary means of communication, any opportunities for friction through conflict will also be greatly reduced. In an ideal parallel parenting arrangement, parents will only interact with one another for necessary scheduling and decision-making situations, meaning that any opportunities for conflict are greatly limited.

- Reduced Interference:

Parallel parenting means letting go of control over how your ex is parenting. Think of it as a business arrangement. This can be hard. It might mean having to bristle to yourself overhearing how your child has been allowed to stay up all night or download the newest video game that you wanted them not to play. It means no more "Why did you let them … ?" phone calls. Difficult as it is, parallel parenting means letting go of an element of that control. Not all the control. Big decisions still need to be jointly decided (ideally through your choice of mediator). But for the small things, it is trusting that your co-parent, even if you might not agree with their choices, is in charge of their allocated parenting time.

- Improved Well-Being and Development of Children:

With parents spending less time yelling at each other on the phone or in person, it is a win-win for everyone; primarily the children, who will no longer have to deal with parents at each other's throats or find themselves getting dragged into fights. This means a healthier, happier, and calmer environment for everyone involved – most importantly, your children.

How to Create a Parallel Parenting Plan

Agreeing on a detailed plan is most likely to reduce stress through setting realistic goals and expectations from both parents. This is most easily accomplished with the help of a third-party mediator (or divorce lawyer in some cases). Ideal parallel parenting plans should include many elements of a co-parenting plan, with some more concrete distinctions:

- Establishing how often each parent will see the child
- Agreeing on concrete times and durations of visits in writing, or using a calendar model that both parents can access
- Planning which parent will host on birthdays and holidays far in advance

- Determining how canceled visits will be dealt with, and how the parents will communicate the need for cancellations
- Finding a neutral method of picking up and dropping off, for example asking a family member or friend to do so to avoid face-to-face interactions if needed
- Setting out clear financial duties for each parent

Tips for Successful Parallel Parenting

Parallel parenting can seem incredibly difficult at first. However, these are a few of the elements which you can incorporate to maintain success in a parallel parenting situation.

1. Prioritize Your Own Needs:

After the end of a particularly turbulent relationship, chances are you would rather block, delete, move on with your life, and never hear from them again. This is however rarely an option when children are involved. Nonetheless, even when actively working to construct a working relationship with a parallel parent, you must conserve an element of kindness to yourself. Prioritize other forms of self-care, whatever that may mean to you; whether it is shopping, gaming, hot baths, or binge-watching your favorite shows. Reducing your stress levels will bolster you enough to deal with the highs and lows of parallel parenting in the long run.

2. Accept the Current Situation:

It is not going to be easy (and if it is, you are amongst the very, very lucky ones). It can be easy to get stuck in a negative thought cycle of what-ifs, and build up resentment, regret, and anger toward your ex, and probably a bit of shame yourself. However, harboring these emotions will only impact you negatively further in the future. Seeking therapy where possible, and if not, finding methods to actively practice acceptance on your own are positive outlets for working on accepting your current situation, and in doing so, allocating the maximum amount of care and priority to your children.

3. Keep Communication to the Minimum:

As stressed above, parallel parenting relationships operate most successfully when communication is at a minimum; no late-night texts, no early weekend calls about what your child's schedule is going to look like, no forwarding memes, and no using your child to relay information to their other parent. Communicate only when necessary, and when that is the case, through the appropriate methods outlined in your parenting plan.

4. Appoint a Mediator:

Asking for help can be difficult. Trusting someone else to make good decisions, especially when it involves your children, is also incredibly difficult. However, incorporating a third-party mediator into parallel parenting relationships is one of the keys to success (particularly in the early stages), when you both struggle to communicate. Mediators can range from family members to friends, to lawyers and counselors, to a range of modern solutions such as apps and calendarizing technology.

Parallel Parenting With a Toxic Co-Parent

Parallel parenting is hard enough as it is. Trying to do so successfully with a toxic parent is setting you off ten steps back. Individuals with toxic or narcissistic tendencies will be more likely to lash out and make bids to take full control. They may use prior knowledge of how you operate and personal information to their advantage to try and attack your character. As difficult as it is, moving forward with a parallel parenting plan as calmly and collectedly as possible will relinquish any power this toxic individual holds over you and detract from the attention they are trying to gain for themselves.

Keys to Successfully Parallel Parenting With a Toxic Parent:

Successful parallel parenting with a toxic parent might require a few of the adjustments listed below to allow you to do so most effectively. If at first, you do not succeed, do not be afraid of making adjustments down the line.

- Set Expectations:

Parallel parenting is unfortunately not just a learn-as-you-go type of situation. It involves having firm boundaries in place, set out by a third-party mediator, and a clear plan of how parental custody is to be divided in terms of time each parent spends with the child, and how the child should be transferred from one parent to another. Dates, times, and durations should all be set out in writing, and consequences for failure to comply with turning up or dropping off at the agreed times should also be included, such as escalating the situation to legal representatives or law enforcement.

- Maintain Strict Boundaries:

Healthy boundaries are needed in any relationship but are paramount to succeeding in parenting alongside a particularly caustic and selfish individual. As difficult as it may be, honoring your agreement with one another to parent separately and not reaching out to lecture or observe how they are parenting is critical (as long as the welfare and safety of the child are not in any way at stake).

- Detach From the Toxic Parent:

Toxic parents tend to excel in using your own words against you, and as someone you most likely shared a large portion of your life with before your relationship breakdown, they will be armed with a plethora of information on how to get you where it hurts. Minimizing communication and all forms of engagement removes this power from them, protecting both yourself and your child as you relinquish them of the opportunity to lash out.

- Keep Track of Everything:

In parallel parenting with someone who does not have fair interests at heart, keeping a record of every interaction, every pickup, drop off, text screenshots, and even minor details, can avoid any future disagreement to the tone of 'I said/they said.'

- Do Not Feed Their Toxicity:

Getting worked up over texting, calling, and engaging in verbal arguments will often work against you and provide the toxic parent with weaponry to double back and use against you in the future. If you do ever need to engage in communication, take a step back, a deep breath, and send the message to a trusted friend or family member to review beforehand, to avoid showing any weaknesses which might be used against you.

- Stick to a Detailed Plan:

Your parallel parenting plan is more important than ever when dealing with a toxic individual. Toxic people are experts at finding loopholes and seeking out vulnerabilities. Making sure that you do not overlook any potential scenario, and have a plan in place in case of something unexpected, will reduce the potential for any disagreements or future areas of conflict.

- Prepare Yourself for Attacks:

Even in the most organized of parallel parenting plans, it is likely that a truly toxic individual will still find means to lash out and try and find ways to hurt you. Learning certain methods of defense, such as meditation, breathwork, or disengaging, will help you maintain calm and avoid engaging with being baited or personal attacks against your character.

- Prioritize the Well-Being of Your Child:

The heavy conflict between parents can often leave little room for engagement and prioritization for the well-being of the children. De-centering your ex from your thoughts can leave far more space for you to focus on your children, and to create a safe space and home where they know they can trust and confide in you, receiving your undivided attention.

Parenting With an Uncooperative Parent

Ideally, even after separation or divorce, parents would be able to put their differences behind them and focus on the well-being of their children above all. Teamwork is after all dreamwork. However, the reality is often not quite so easy. Wounded individuals will often reflect and return to the past and continue to let it get in the way of building a future successful and healthy co-parenting relationship, by letting their emotions get the better of them.

Is Your Ex Uncooperative or Just Difficult?

It can be easy to view regular disagreements and conflict as a refusal to engage and cooperate. These are however likely occurrences, especially in a parallel or co-parenting relationship in its early stages. Learning to parent after a separation or divorce is a long and difficult road – a rollercoaster, even, with lots of ups and downs. Conflict, in the beginning, is almost unavoidable but is not the same as a complete refusal to cooperate down the line.

- Is Your Ex Refusing to Cooperate in all Areas or Is It an Isolated Situation?

Sometimes, refusal to engage will be limited to one area. For example, your co-parent might be willing to modify payment contributions and supplement paying for extracurricular activities but will double down and refuse to cooperate when it comes to adjusting holiday schedules or accommodating different school pickup times. Assessing the limits of how much cooperation (or lack thereof) is actively in place can help to work through issues and use what is working to your advantage.

- What Works for Some Does Not Work for Others:

Parallel parenting is not a one-size-fits-all situation. Certain setups that you have heard about from your friends in similar situations might not work for you. Using an app, for example, might not work for you whilst it does for some. Asking a family member to step in might also lead to some conflicts of interest. Testing different methods until you find one that works is often the best solution to finding the most agreeable solution to your situation.

Potential Areas of Conflict and How to Manage

Conflict is often best mitigated when every possibility is planned for, and you've looked far enough ahead to consider every 'what if?' The following are scenarios in which conflict might arise, and it is worth considering how you would respond to each situation.

- Expenses:

Disagreements over monetary expenses and responsibilities can lead to a great deal of conflict. There are, however, an increasing number of solutions that allow parents to keep track of expenses and invoices, ranging from basic Excel sheets to a wide range of joint expense apps to help you work out your required contributions.

- Scheduling:

Scheduling disagreements can cause a huge deal of conflict, and even minor miscommunications over scheduling may cause huge flare-ups. Using basic methods of planning such as written calendars or texted reminders will often not be enough to handle the schedules of the lives of two individuals parenting separately, as well as one or more children. Resorting to more organized methods of scheduling systems such as certain apps will likely lessen the burden of coordinating the timetables of three or more people, and reduce any potential for miscommunication about allocated time with children, pick-ups, drop-offs, appointments, and holidays.

How to Handle an Uncooperative Parallel Parent

If you have reached a stage of healing where you can look toward the future, put your past aside, and are trying to focus on creating the best environment for your children but find yourself up against a toxic and uncooperative co-parent, it can be incredibly disheartening. However, do not let this stop you from trying to make the most of your situation.

- Accept That You Cannot Change Your Parallel Parent:

Spending time stressing over how you want to change your parallel parent will only lead to unnecessary stress. These things are beyond your control, and as much as you might like to change their behavior and how they present themselves as a person, this will be a fruitless venture. As difficult as it is, accepting that your parallel parent is showing up for your child in their way – whatever that they mean – is the key to finding solace and peace in your new arrangement.

- Set Healthy Boundaries and Be Consistent for Your Child:

It can be tempting to try and one-up your parallel parent when you hear about them giving your child the newest toys and gadgets, taking them to movies you do not think that they should be seeing yet, and letting them stay up late. Avoid trying to engage in a rat race and compete to be the better, more loved parent. Setting clear rules and discipline is something that your children will benefit from down the line.

- Set Up a Parenting Plan:

For a parallel parent refusing to engage and cooperate, a clear and concise parenting plan set up by a third-party mediator will likely encourage both parties to adhere to clear rules and instructions set out for them. Consequences for failing to comply will also increase the chances of active participation.

- Do Not Allow Yourself to Be Manipulated:

Particularly when dealing with an uncooperative parallel parent, you might find yourself tempted to bend and sway to their requests and desires. Of course, leniency is required to some degree, but maintaining your boundaries is also critical. Setting the tone for your requirements and sticking by them is paramount to maintaining respect on both sides and not allowing yourself to be manipulated by negative behaviors.

- Silence Is the Best Answer:

Silence is often the best response to any antagonistic attacks. Not always, but choosing not to flare up and react to an ex who is trying to push your buttons is most frequently the best response. Quite often, a toxic individual who is looking to provoke you is seeking that reaction. You maintain your superiority and your power by taking a step back and a deep breath and choosing not to rise to their taunts.

- Be Sure Not to Criticize Your Co-Parent Behind Their Back:

It can be tempting to criticize your parallel parent to your children. Children are however incredibly conscious of everything spoken in the environment around them and influenced by both how you present yourself and your opinions. Avoid dragging your children into a war against your parallel parent as this will burden them emotionally, and instead avoid any form of negative talk surrounding your parallel parent when in the presence of your children.

- Build a Support Network:

Parallel parenting is difficult. It is made ten times more difficult in the presence of an uncooperative parent. Where possible, find people that you can confide in, like therapists, friends, family, and support groups. Finding a safe space in which you can vent freely and receive advice will likely lessen the burden and frustration building up in trying to deal with an uncooperative parallel parent. It is, however, critical that you do not share too much information with an individual who has ties to both you and your ex, as this may present as a conflict of interest if they relay back to your ex.

Reflective Questions

1. *Your ex sends you several heated text messages late at night, degrading your parenting style. What methods can you use to take a step back and help yourself not engage with these messages?*

2. *Your parallel parent cancels hosting your children for the weekend at the last minute. What policy do you have in place to deal with cancellations?*

3. *Your ex is refusing to contribute to their share of school costs. How do you deal with this?*

Summary

In this chapter, we have covered the benefits of parallel parenting; for those who struggle with co-parenting, and need to set out a structured and formal business-like arrangement to continue parenting in the best way possible for their children.

You have learned how to set out a structured plan, minimize contact to reduce conflict, and incorporate a mediator to help you. You also have learned how to set out a parallel parenting plan with a toxic, narcissistic, or uncooperative parent, to prioritize the well-being of your children above everything.

In the next chapter, we will cover how to deal with loyalty conflicts that children might experience during or post-divorce.

Chapter 6:
Loyalty Conflicts

"When mom and dad went to war, the only prisoners they took were their children."

— Pat Conroy

One of my mom's friends got a divorce in her early fifties. She has two boys, who were aged 8 and 14 at the time. The divorce came as a result of many factors but was mainly because she and her ex-husband had just drifted apart after so many years together. There was no animosity between them, and they were very content to part ways as friends. However, their eldest son had a hard time processing the separation. He was angry, he wanted someone to blame, and he chose his father. He began to lash out at his dad during their time spent together. He acted out at home, staying up late and slamming doors, or not coming home at all.

His dad met someone new and tried to introduce her to his children after several months. The eldest son became angrier than ever and refused to even leave his mom's house. At this point, his dad began to also get angry and would phone his ex-wife and demand to know what she had been saying to her son that would cause him to blame him.

She was at a loss. The divorce had been a mutual agreement, and she very much wanted her sons to have a healthy relationship with their dad. She had been avoiding the topic of her ex-husband in her house because it was a trigger for so much anger in her boys. However, she sat down and tried to get to the bottom of why her eldest son was so furious with his dad. It had gotten to the point where she had to talk to both sons, as the youngest was beginning to mimic his brother by showing signs of hostility toward his father.

After a long discussion, she concluded that they both thought that their father had begun seeing his new girlfriend whilst they were still married and were certain this was the reason that they had been forced to move school and leave all of their friends behind. She was angry with herself for not having sat down and talked through their feelings earlier, but was able to reassure both her boys that this was not the case, that she and her ex-husband had moved on from one another with no hard feelings, that he had remained loyal up until their divorce, and that she wanted them to repair their relationship with their father as she still thought so much of her ex-husband.

What is a Loyalty Conflict?

Watching parents break up is incredibly difficult for children. We grow up in a society where happy nuclear families are put on a pedestal, and the sudden separation of the two most important people in a child's life can cause immense stress. It can also lead children to feel torn about whether to align themselves closer to one parent over the other. They might blame one parent more for causing the divorce and tearing their lives apart. They might also be in a stage of life where they feel closer to one parent for no obvious reason, and thus push the other away. They might attempt to show loyalty to the parent they feel has been treated poorly by the divorce by lashing out against their other parent, and pushing them away. Whilst this inner emotional turmoil is happening, they will also be likely to experience extreme emotional conflicts within, as they naturally yearn for their parents to get back together.

Supporting a child who is experiencing loyalty conflicts after a divorce is incredibly complex, made even more difficult if their other parent encourages parental alienation and heightens their feelings of anger and resentment.

Children are more vulnerable to loyalty conflicts than adults, as they have yet to develop their emotional intelligence and broader view of the world. They will often struggle to understand the bigger picture of their parents' divorce and the reasons behind it, as well as the nuances of married life. Children of a young age also struggle to verbalize and articulate their feelings, as well as what type of support and reassurance they require. They might be unable to ask the right questions and instead withdraw completely from the situation, with their inaccurate picture of why their parents chose to divorce, and whom they should blame. They might even stray as far as to blame themselves, and feel guilty and torn about how to respond to both parents who now live in a completely foreign, separated living situation.

What Causes a Loyalty Conflict?

Loyalty conflicts are not uncommon after a divorce. The reasons behind them can vary, but below are potential scenarios in which a child might begin to feel divided between parents.

- Child Experiences Loyalty Conflict Between Separated Parents:

Children will often experience the consequences of emotional conflict between their parents post-divorce, even if the parents are doing their utmost to hide this strife. They might choose to side with one parent over the other due to witnessing their parents argue and criticize their ex; "If your dad had not slept with his co-worker, this whole mess would not have happened. He is a horrible person," or "This whole divorce only happened because your mom is an awful parent. If only she had spent more time at home and less time at work."

Statements like these often force a child into believing that they have to side with one parent over the other, as they will otherwise struggle to maintain neutrality when met with their parents condemning one another – particularly when they come to see one parent as having caused the divorce.

Children will occasionally also create loyalty conflicts by passing their judgment over the situation, even when unaware of what exactly caused the divorce; "I do not know exactly why my parents are getting a divorce, but I am sure it is because of Mom's (or Dad's) drinking/anger/affair. I hate her (or him)." This is particularly prevalent in older children and teenagers who are more likely to resort to anger and resentment as a way of dealing with their feelings.

Arguing with your ex in the presence of your children, talking badly about them, or using your children as messengers for sending hostile messages from one home to the other will likely amplify feelings of anger or loyalty conflicts within children, and should be avoided where possible.

- Child Experiences Loyalty Conflict Toward New Stepparent Versus Biological Parent:

When the time comes for new partners to be introduced, loyalty conflicts will likely arise as children might feel guilty for building a bond with a new stepparent, and avoid doing so out of loyalty to their biological parent. For instance, a child might be aggravated by their father introducing a new stepmother figure, and feel injustice on behalf of their biological mother. Perhaps their father was unfaithful, causing the divorce, and the child blames their father entirely. Perhaps their biological mother even eggs on their hatred for their stepmother. They laugh together about the wicked witch of the West, who has moved into their father's apartment and set their lives on fire.

Although difficult as it may be, avoiding staking the flames of initial loyalty conflicts a child may be experiencing will do better in the long run. Putting your resentment toward your ex might be difficult, as might be speaking well of their new partner. Where possible, avoid the topic altogether, or engage with your children in a passive and non-reactive manner.

- Parent Feels Guilty and Makes it Up by Permissive Parenting:

A biological parent might feel guilty for having caused the divorce or separation and might try and make it up to their children by treating them to everything their heart desires. This will often involve straying off the parenting plan, letting them stay up late and eat ice cream until they burst. In turn, being allowed to run wild at one parent's house will leave the child feeling sore and aggrieved when they have to return to the strict rules of their other parent's house. This itself can cause a conflict of loyalty, as despite one parent considering themselves more to blame for the divorce, they buy the favor of their children by treating them so leniently, often causing them to resent the parent who follows a more structured schedule.

Early Warning Signs of Loyalty Conflicts

Whilst children's affection towards each parent might appear to flourish then wane, keep an eye out for extreme cases which might signify an early loyalty conflict that your child is experiencing.

- Constant Attacks:

Children suddenly behaving in a continuously negative manner toward you is a sign that they have chosen to blame you over their other parent. This might manifest in a constant stream of verbal belittlements and attacks of character, and refusing to listen or engage with anything you say. They will probably criticize you over even the smallest of things, and bring up any and every occasion in the past in which you have had a conflict with one another. This will probably look like a small campaign against your character, within the confines of your own home.

- Idealizing One Parent:

A child who fully engages in a conflict of loyalty might place one parent on a pedestal, and the other in the gutters. They will be unable to act or see rationally when it comes to visualizing either parent. Any actions the hero performs are gallant and to be praised, whilst anything the parent they resent does will be met with outright fury. They might completely refuse to see the parent they are choosing to blame. They might also make their feelings on the subject very vocal by attacking one parent and showing steadfast loyalty and protectiveness over the other parent.

- Parroting:

Does something your child says to you, perhaps a particularly hurtful statement, sound like something that came instead from the lips of your ex? Your child might come up with not only paraphrased attacks but also baseless accusations that they might have overheard. Parroting attacks are made far worse by a toxic parent that encourages this behavior, even giving them statements to relay to their less-favored parent.

- Blind Support for Favored Parent:

In the eyes of a child who is in the midst of a loyalty crisis, the favored parent can often do no wrong. They will side with them in situations of conflict where it is even beyond common sense to do so. In their eyes, the favored parent is always in the right, and they are willing to fight for them in any arguments that might arise.

- Lack of Respect:

A child experiencing a conflict of loyalty will often show no remorse for treating you poorly, throwing insults your way, or misbehaving in your household. Your authority as a parent will be erased, and they might act out whilst in your presence as a way to demonstrate their loyalty to their other parent. They might also withdraw emotionally, forgetting their manners and gratitude.

- Extending Anger to Your Close Circle:

Not only does your child now blame you for the divorce but shows it daily. They hate Grandma now too. Your grandma, that is. Anyone associated with or related to you gets blacklisted. By extension, they might try to demonstrate a fierce loyalty to one parent by rejecting anyone and everyone close to them.

A child cutting off one biological parent, whether willingly or not, will often lead to impaired feelings of self-worth and other behavioral issues. Therefore, preventing this from happening is often in the best interest of children – unless the parent in question is engaging in dangerous behavior themselves.

How Loyalty Conflicts Affect Children

Loyalty conflicts can be very difficult to deal with, taking an emotional toll both on your child and yourself. If you find yourself on the receiving end, or trying to support a child undergoing these feelings, try and remain empathetic to what they're going through.

- Feelings of Guilt and Pressure to Choose One Parent Over the Other:

Although in an ideal world, children will come out of the other side of their parents' divorce and be able to continue channeling the same level of love and devotion to each parent, this is often far from reality. Frequently, children can end up feeling pressured to choose between their parents. They might blame one parent for causing the divorce more so than the other. They might also see one parent fueling more of the arguments during the custody battle and start to feel like they need to protect the less confrontational parent. All of these require a role reversal of the parent-child relationship, in which feelings of guilt and resentment will build up in the child, often causing subsequent issues such as anger or anxiety.

Additionally, if after a divorce a child feels unable to please both parents simultaneously, this will almost undoubtedly cause a loyalty conflict out of anxiousness to maintain some level of consistent love and reassurance, if only from one side. It must be made clear to the child that both parents will continue to love and support them, no matter what, to avoid them being pressured into a situation where they feel forced to choose one parent over the other.

Parents can also encourage loyalty conflicts, sometimes on purpose, by talking poorly about their co-parent in the presence of their child. Children are easily influenced by their parents, and one parent speaking negatively about the other may often leave children doubting their bond with the parent that is being criticized.

- Losing Respect for Parents and Their Parenting Ability:

"If my parents could not even keep their marriage together, how could they possibly have the skills needed to look after me properly?"

It is not an uncommon worry in the minds of children of divorce. Seeing their parents expend all of their energy on arguing with one another over putting effort into healthy parenting will increase these feelings of doubt about their parenting capabilities. This can potentially cause them to withdraw from the relationship with one or both parents, as well as have possible behavioral consequences for the child, such as anxiousness.

- Impacts Trust in Future Relationships:

Children who have had to find their way through parental loyalty conflicts will often find it hard to trust individuals in romantic and friendship settings as they get older. If they watched the decline of their parents' marriage, they might doubt that they will ever be able to have a successful marriage themselves, so might abstain entirely.

They will often cocoon themselves away from letting people get close to them, as a way of protecting themselves from the hurt that they witnessed during the divorce.

How to Avoid Loyalty Conflicts

Loyalty conflicts are not uncommon following a divorce or separation, so it is best to plan ahead. Even if you and your ex get along fine and your children seem at ease with you both, have a contingency plan in place in case anything else should arise.

- Set Up a Parenting Plan:

As we have covered, a well-structured and expansive parenting plan will mean that children have less doubt when it comes to elements that might cause loyalty conflicts; such as where they are spending the holidays, or what time they are allowed to go to bed. Children will also feel less guilty about choosing to spend time with one parent over the other if this choice is made for them.

When possible, being on the same page as your co-parent and having set out your expectations clearly and in agreement with one another will mean that your children feel less inclined to side with one parent over the other and are thus less likely to experience a loyalty conflict.

- Reassurance:

Remember to tell your child that you love them, no matter what. Be sure to work regularly on reinforcing your parent-child relationship, through verbalizing your affection regularly, or whichever way they hear it best; whether quality time spent together or showing an interest in their hobbies. A child who feels like both parents support and love them equally will be less likely to start feeling that one parent loves them more than the other.

- Parallel Parenting:

For high-conflict families who find themselves unable to follow through with co-parenting, parallel parenting can help reduce loyalty conflicts by formulating a still strict plan, but far less communication, so that mom and dad are arguing less in front of the children, making them privy to less stress. The less conflict, the less inclined children feel to have to side with one parent or the other or protect a parent, therefore less likely to find themselves in any form of loyalty conflict.

- Mediators:

As getting a court date to sort out every argument is often an unlikely prospect, many states have formulated programs whereby attorneys and mental health services are involved in post-divorce disagreements. Third-party mediators can help parents come to an agreement over issues of conflict and resolve them swiftly. This often helps speed up the process of a separated family finding their feet after a divorce and leaves children feeling more comfortable in their new lives. Where possible, involving a family counselor or therapist can also help unify divorced parents and sort out smaller issues and help children understand their feelings.

- Prioritize Children:

A point that cannot be stressed enough; putting the well-being of your children above your feelings will inevitably make them feel reassured and supported, even in the upheaval after a divorce. Their welfare should be your priority, and in doing so, you should avoid speaking ill of your ex in their presence. Whatever feelings you might still have, need to be put to one side so that you can create a safe and non-reactive environment in which your children can find their feet after a divorce, and avoid falling into any loyalty conflicts in siding with one parent over the other.

- Encourage the Involvement of the Co-Parent:

Parenting alone after a divorce is a difficult road, although it might seem tempting at first – particularly if you want to avoid being in regular communication with your ex. However, as we have covered, children benefit most from the involvement of both parents, so it is key that you remain neutral toward your co-parent when possible, and encourage their involvement in your child's life.

You can still avoid incorporating too much of your ex into your own life if you need to do so for your healing purposes. You need not ask your children what they got up to with them over the weekend, or how your co-parent is doing in their own life, particularly in a situation of high conflict or whilst parallel parenting where you have requested a low level of communication.

Whatever your plan might be, maintaining the mindset that your children will benefit most from growing up with both parents, even if this is harder for you, is key to helping them feel less guilty over aligning themselves more with one parent over the other.

Loyalty Bind Talks With Children

Communication is the best first step to helping a child work through feelings of guilt or divided loyalty between parents. If you notice your child exhibiting signs of a loyalty conflict, try and speak with them in person and explore their feelings, assuring them that they are loved by both parents and that you are understanding of the difficulties they are going through.

- Reinforce that the child is not to blame for the divorce.
- Reassure your child that they will always be loved, no matter what.
- Reiterate that your child remains your priority, and you'll be working together as parents to repair their life.

Example:

"I know that you blame your dad for the divorce because he asked for it when I was not ready and I was angry at the time. That does not mean that it was not the right thing for us to do. When two adults do not love each other anymore the way that they need to, the best solution is getting a divorce. That does not mean that we do not both love you. Of course, we do and always will. It also does not mean that we both do not love and appreciate each other as friends. We want to work together to build a new life, where we live separately and move on to our own lives, but can still support you in the best way possible."

Additional Examples of Ways to Reassure Children

- "I am sorry that you had to see Mom and Dad fighting so much. I know it must have been upsetting, but you do not have to worry about us. We are sorting out the adult stuff and we love you regardless."

- "I know that you feel angry about Mom seeing a new partner, but I hope you can come to welcome your stepdad. You are not expected to love him the same way that you love me, which both your stepdad and I know."

- "You have been so strong and brave during this divorce. I know that you saw me upset about it during the weekend, but that does not mean you should take it out on your dad during your time together. Go and enjoy the rest of the week – I am excited to see you when you get back but I want you to make the most of your time with Dad!"

Reflective Questions

1. *Throughout your relationship, your ex made numerous comments about how they think you don't exercise enough. Your child suddenly starts making similar comments when they are alone with you. How do you bring up where this statement has come from?*

2. Nothing you do is right. Your children berate you for your cooking, your attention span, and your appearance. You're met with a steady stream of criticism. What's your first step in getting to the bottom of where this is coming from? How do you calm yourself if you feel vulnerable and upset at the critique?

3. You have a new partner. Your children show increasing animosity toward you and seem defensive of their other parent. How can you best explain the introduction of your new partner? Is it possible to get your ex on board?

Summary

In this chapter, we have covered loyalty conflicts and how they manifest in children of divorce; what causes children to feel pressured to side with one parent over the other, reject a new stepparent, or begin to side with whichever parent is more lenient in their parenting. We have also explored the long-term negative effects of loyalty conflicts in children, and how to work together as co-parents to prevent them from arising.

In cases of parenting alongside a toxic ex, it can often be more difficult to prevent loyalty conflicts. We will explore the consequences of this in the next chapter: parental alienation.

Chapter 7:
Parental Alienation

Parental alienation is an emotional act of violence that is aimed at an adult, but critically wounds a child."

— Steve Maraboli

I made a friend at one of the parenting classes I took several years ago. She was a kind woman who was often quiet and said little when it came to sharing with the class. It took a while for her to trust me and open up about her own experience with parental alienation.

She had held sole custody over her son for 12 years. His father remained a background figure in his life; moving addresses, forgetting birthdays, and ignoring his child support duties until he remarried. The father, alongside his new wife, had suddenly reappeared in the boy's life, and they were desperate to take full control. She told me that her son was hesitant at first. After all, he did not know his father at all. He was still a stranger to him. But first came the gifts. Then games, clothes and toys. The car was the turning point. He could not even legally drive. His mother had told him he had to wait until he could legally drive. All it took was one grand gesture, and the boy was gone.

His dad had gradually wormed his way more into the boy's life. Her son began to refuse to return to her house when he was supposed to and told her that he much preferred the freedom his father and his new stepmother granted him. They let him stay up late on school nights, go to parties, and bought him alcohol to impress his friends. This came at a cost. He had to stop calling and texting his mom, and as it later transpired, to get these gifts, he had to tell her himself that he no longer wanted to spend his time with her. He became bitter and cold when they were together, sometimes shouting about how his dad had told him what he claimed to be the truth; that his mother had forbidden him from seeing him all these years, and that she was a callous and selfish person for stealing him away.

After 12 years of raising the boy on her own, his mother was distraught. She watched her relationship with her son crumble for several months before she took a stand. She tells me how much she regrets not acting sooner, and I can see the pain on her face. She attends parenting classes now, once a week, as she agreed to in court. It took her a long time before she hired an attorney, and her face crumples as she tells me about how long and tiresome the process was. She had to remind herself that she was not fighting her son, whom she loved so dearly, but the man whom she had not seen for over a decade, and the new woman in his life. Still, I can hear the pain in her voice when she explains how the court set out new terms and rules in their parenting agreement, and how when ordered to spend allocated periods with her, her son would often refuse to get out of his dad's car to even come and see her.

Still, she tells me that life has improved. She is not a bitter person. She seems happy that she now is back in contact with her son, even if that means sharing him with someone who waged such a painful war against her character and stole away the little boy she worked so hard to raise on her own.

What is Parental Alienation?

Parental alienation is a process through which a parent tries to turn a child against their other parent through intentional manipulation and unjustified negativity.

Parental Alienation Versus Estrangement

Some cases of a child rejecting their parent are not down to the manipulation or brainwashing of the other parent. It is worth knowing the difference, to avoid pointing fingers and to also understand how to best support a child experiencing or displaying one of the following signs of parental estrangement:

- Separation Anxiety:

This is particularly prevalent in unequal custodial arrangements, where one parent sees far more of a child. When it comes to having to spend time with the parent who has secondary custody, young children, in particular, will act visibly anxious and distressed towards the change. This might result in temper tantrums or other ways of acting out, much in the same way little ones will quake with fear on their first day of school, or be alarmed at the introduction of a new babysitter.

Even for older children who spend most of their time with their mom, having to go to their dad's place for a weekend might seem like a confusing and scary prospect that they would rather avoid altogether.

- Poor Parenting:

If a child views the relationship that they have with their parent negatively or feels that their needs go unmet in the care of that parent, it is unlikely that they will be overly keen at the prospect of spending time with them. A parent who never has food in the house, spends all their day on the computer or forgets to pick them up from school might find themselves with children who would rather forego spending time at their house. Equally, a parent who is overly strict and resorts to shouting might also find that their children would rather stay at the home of the parent they consider calmer and more amiable.

- Rebellion:

Teens and pre-teens going through hormonal changes might just come to project their mood swings upon one parent over the other. A sullen 14-year-old who refuses to come down for breakfast and glowers at you when you try and ask them about their day may well just be going through some developmental shifts as opposed to reacting to what their other parent has said or done.

- Extreme Punishment and Discipline:

Divorced co-parents agreeing on shared expectations for discipline is especially important as otherwise, it is not unlikely that the children will come to favor the more lenient parent. If in one house, the children are slapped for not listening to rules or have their phones taken away for not eating their vegetables, the children might decide to avoid going to stay with that parent altogether. Aggressive methods of punishment will understandably lead to children resent being afraid of a parent.

- Outside Factors:

Numerous other factors can lead to a child rejecting a parent of their own accord after a divorce. If one parent is substantially better off financially than the other, and lives in a bigger house, with a nicer car, and better food, the children might find themselves more inclined to stay with that parent. The influence of their friends might also come into play, with them feeling ashamed of having to admit that one parent now lives in a poorer neighborhood, in a tiny apartment. Additionally, children might come to reject the new partners of their parents, leaving them unwilling to spend time with that parent.

- Parental Issues:

Even if a parent had no issues before a divorce, the emotional upheaval might leave them vulnerable to negative behaviors such as addictions. Children might reject a parent who has started drinking excessively or gambling.

Types of Alienating Parents

Psychologist Douglas Darnall identified three types of parental alienators in his 1999 study.

1. Naive Alienators:

Parents who are passive about the relationship their children hold with their other parent but occasionally say something negative about that parent fall into this category. Even well-meaning parents might fall into this category on occasion, without truly wanting to turn their child against the other parent.

2. Active Alienators:

Parents who are more inclined to emotional outbursts, who might still feel hurt by the divorce and resentful towards their ex, and who react to triggers by losing control of their behavior fall into this category. They tend also to want their child to continue having a relationship with the other parent, but sometimes let their emotions get the better of them.

3. Obsessed Alienators:

The category for toxic exes and co-parents; obsessed alienators are unable to put the well-being of their children above their mission to destroy the reputation of their ex in the eyes of their children. They set out on a crusade to destroy the relationship their children have with their other parent and try to manipulate and turn the children against them. They might believe their ex to be an unfit and abusive parent or are simply just desperate enough to make things up to support their vendetta.

When Does Parental Alienation Happen?

You know your ex very well. You should be able to tell what type of person they are, and if they are the sort to actively start trying to alienate your children against you. This will be different from the occasional criticism of one another. In the early days after a divorce, you might also find yourself acting as a naive alienator and saying carelessly negative things about your co-parent. However, remain alert if you know your ex is the sort of person to try and manipulate your children against you, and you think that one of the following situations applies to them:

- When One Parent Is Not Over the Divorce and Tries to Lash Out at the Other Parent:

Someone who is still riled up about divorce and has not processed their feelings might lash out and try to emotionally hurt the other parent by turning their children against them.

- When a Parent Develops False Beliefs About the Other's Parenting Skills:

If a parent believes their ex is unfit for parenting on their own, they might act out by trying to alienate their children against the other parent. Perhaps they believe their co-parent does not have enough time to parent successfully. Perhaps they think that their co-parent is too strict, and engages in physical discipline. Whatever the reason, this parent might believe that they are acting in the best interests of their children by encouraging them to reject the parent that they see as unfit for parenting.

- When a Parent Fears Losing Their Children:

Having already lost so much during a divorce, a parent might act out of fear of also losing their children. They might believe that their ex will soon attempt to alienate their children against them, thus believing that by acting out first, they are protecting themselves and their relationship with their children.

- When a Parent Is Mentally Unwell:

An individual suffering from a mental illness such as a personality disorder might become overly paranoid about the involvement of their co-parent and their capabilities. This might involve a degree of delusion and obsession.

Techniques That Parental Alienators Use

Parental alienators sit in one of the most extreme categories of toxic exes. They will employ all the techniques they know for manipulating and criticizing you, to draw your children away from you and turn them against you. You might have noticed some of these techniques being used against you during your marriage or relationship, so it is worth remembering that if you were once manipulated, controlled, or gaslit, your co-parent might begin to use these very same techniques on your children.

- Criticizing and Badmouthing:

Parents who are attempting to alienate their children will often engage in a constant stream of verbal or non-verbal criticism against the other parent. This might be based on pre-existing flaws or completely fabricated. In either case, a parental figure whom the child trusts constantly degrading their other parent will cause the child to question and doubt that individual.

- Telling the Child That Their Other Parent Does Not Love Them:

Even if children feel that they are loved and supported by both parents, being constantly told that they are not loved by a trusted figure will foster feelings of doubt and insecurity. The alienating parent might go as far as to say that the entire divorce is down to the other parent not loving the child. Statements like "Daddy does not love you anymore. He has left you," or "If mom did love you, she would never have asked for a divorce," will result in a child starting to feel reservations about whether or not they are loved and appreciated.

- Telling the Child That Their Other Parent Is Dangerous or Unfit to Parent:

An alienating parent might attempt to convince a child that their other parent is incapable of parenting by creating a false narrative about how the parent is toxic. They might use old memories or experiences and spin them to the child in a deceitful manner, telling the child that their parent hurt or attempted to hurt them. They might also criticize the other parent's parenting style, saying that they do not have the child's best interests at heart, that they cannot provide a safe home, and that they have monetary issues, a criminal record, or substance abuse issues.

- Restricting Visitation:

A parent who is attempting to alienate a child might ignore any agreements set out by the court and custody. They might refuse to let the child leave their home and go to their other parent as agreed upon in their schedule, or try and bribe them to decide for themselves; "How about you do not go to your mother's place this weekend, and I will take you to a theme park instead?" A child will naturally start to believe more that is said by the parent with whom they spend the most time, thus an alienating parent will try and be the dominant figure in their lives, leaving the child more hesitant around the targeted parent.

- Exposing the Child to the Conflict Between Parents:

We have stressed the importance of not exposing your children to post-divorce conflict, as this can lead to loyalty conflicts and other behavioral issues in children. Parental alienators will try to use this to their advantage. They will try and involve the child in parental disagreements, arguments, and general issues regarding the divorce.

- Forcing the Child to Choose Sides:

Parental alienators might guilt trip children into choosing sides, telling them that they can only receive their love if they deny their other parent. They might also force the child to actively reject their other parent through coercion and bribery. If the other parent feels that their child is choosing not to spend the allocated custody time with them, they might in turn become angry and lash out at the child, which will lead to even more resentment and create a negative circle of rejection and bitterness until the child becomes completely alienated.

- Changing the Child's Name:

A committed alienator might go as far as to change their child's name. Perhaps a mother will revert to her maiden name and will change her child's name as well. She might also remarry and begin using her new husband's surname for the child. A parental alienator of either gender might attempt to legally change the name of the child and use this on all forms of professional records such as medical forms.

- Forcing the Child to Spy on the Other Parent:

A child might be put into a tricky situation where the parental alienator asks them to spy on the other parent. This might include asking them what their parent is getting up to, how they are behaving themselves, or how much they are earning. They might go as far as to ask the child to find legal documents, pay slips, or medical records, and to procure them as evidence. This might be done with a degree of bribery; "If we find out how much Mom made last year, maybe we can ask her to buy you those new shoes that you want!" Even after the first time a child successfully spies on their other parent and informs the alienator, they will begin to feel guilty and remorseful, and less comfortable in the parent that they have betrayed, which will further any feelings of rejection.

- Forcing the Child to Refer to and See the New Stepparent as 'Mom' or 'Dad':

A parental alienator might be swift to bring new partners into their life and position them as a replacement for their co-parent. They might start calling them 'mommy' or 'daddy' in the presence of the child and ask that the child does the same. They might also introduce their new partner as the biological mother or father of the child to important figures such as teachers or parents of friends.

- Asking the Child to Keep Secrets From the Other Parent:

Parental alienators will also use secrecy to distance the child from their other parent. They will request that information that should otherwise be shared with the other parent be kept for them, for example, "I know that you want to go to the beach house this summer. I will take you, but let us not tell Daddy because he will try to stop us."

- Bribery:

In a bid to buy the devotion of their children, alienators might attempt to win them over by buying them new toys, and new clothes, or taking them out on lavish trips. They might also be overly lenient and begin to engage in permissive parenting; allowing their children to roam freely, stay up late, and eat whatever they want as a form of permissive parenting. An alienating parent will know what their child wants and will use it to their advantage to win them over and pit them up against their other parent.

- Guilt-Tripping and Dependency:

As a form of emotional manipulation, a parental alienator might claim that they cannot function without the help of their child. They might beg and deplore, saying that the child is a bad person if they leave them to go and see their other parent. They might be depressed and lonely, or suddenly ill every other week. They will play on the child's feelings of guilt and use them to create an illusion of dependency so that the child feels extreme remorse whenever they leave the alienator.

Signs of Children Experiencing Parental Alienation

The signs that a child is experiencing parental alienation are almost identical to those of a child experiencing a loyalty conflict. Look out for the following in your child's behavior if you are worried they might be falling victim to your ex's manipulation:

- Your child criticizing you regularly
- Your child parroting your ex
- Withdrawing from you emotionally and seemingly unwilling to spend time with you
- Your child losing respect for you and failing to listen to your

authority
- This apparent hatred of you is extended to your relatives and close circle

Effects of Parental Alienation on Children

As we have reinforced the importance of both parents in a child's life, unless a parent poses an immediate danger to a child, the effects of parental alienation and thus losing contact with one parent is profound. Ideally, as parents, you should be working together to unite and prevent this from happening. Nonetheless, it is worth keeping in mind how parental alienation can affect your children if you fall victim, should you need convincing about how hard to fight for your children's sake, or if you feel the temptation to try and cut your ex out of your child's life and need to put a pin in your feelings.

- Dysfunctional Relationships:

Growing up amid a war between parents will lead to a lack of trust in a child. In later life, they might struggle to trust others. This will hold true for friendships and romantic partners; they will have issues with allowing others into their close circle, and worry about those individuals manipulating them or beginning a campaign against their character as they witnessed between their parents. They might also believe that all marriages are doomed, having witnessed the decline of their parents' love for one another and the aftermath, and choose not to engage in marriage themselves out of fear of repeating this pattern.

- Poor Self-Esteem:

A child who is constantly being told that they are not loved by one or more parents will grow up feeling unlovable. This can lead to later life issues such as feelings of unworthiness.

- Behavioral Issues and Mental Health Problems:

Feelings of being unloved as a child can take a major toll and can result in issues such as depression and anxiety, or pushing boundaries and ending up with a criminal record.

- Anxious and Insecure Attachment Style:

Children growing up with a parent who manipulates them and uses them to their advantage might find themselves incredibly anxious when it comes to forming any of their relationships. They will struggle with forming and maintaining boundaries and might engage overly in people-pleasing, or withdraw from socializing and put off forming relationships altogether.

- Academic Impact:

Children who are torn between two parents and begin to suffer at the hands of a parental alienator might find themselves so distracted that they are unable to concentrate at school. Grades might plummet, either because they are too worried or preoccupied, or because they have too much going on at home to care about school.

- Lack of Impulse Control:

As means of escape, victims of parental alienation might turn to drug or alcohol abuse, or other forms of risk-taking behavior.

- Alienation of Own Children:

Unfortunately, history tends to repeat itself. Victims of parental alienation will have a higher tendency to repeat this behavior as adults, as they form and repeat these unhealthy patterns.

How to Protect Your Child Against Parental Alienation

As a parent, if you think that your child is falling victim to your ex's manipulation, you need to act swiftly. Early intervention often helps stop long-term issues with children growing fonder of one parent and cutting off contact with the other – in which, they will solely be in the presence of the alienator and at high risk of losing clear judgment. Be patient, kind, and open-minded, and where possible encourage urge your children to combat negative talk and think freely.

- Encourage Children to Think for Themselves:

Teaching your children to think analytically and to think for themselves will help them think between the black-and-white standards that alienating parents set. They will be more inclined to make up their mind for themselves if they are open-minded and able to analyze the bigger picture. This can include posing questions to your child in their day to day; "What do you think about what has been happening in the news recently?" or "What were your thoughts on this book?"

- Challenge Criticism and Badmouthing:

If you do hear about your ex badmouthing you, do not continuously let it slide. Early intervention will lead to less of an impact of negative statements in the long run. Be sure to respond openly and calmly to your child, and keep in mind that your ex is likely manipulating them to some extent; "I know that Mom told you that I did not come to your match because I do not love you, but that is not true. It was her allocated weekend, and we agreed I would not come. I love you so much and always will."

- Remain Empathetic:

Be aware that your child is likely on the receiving end of a large deal of emotional manipulation and foul play. They might begin to act hostile and defiant in your presence, but where possible, engage in methods to stay calm and composed. Remind yourself that this is an incredibly difficult position for them to be in too. Show that you care and can see how much they are struggling and what a tough time they are going through by using active listening and empathetic phrases to acknowledge their struggles.

- Be Open and Ready to Listen to Your Child:

Children are more likely to fall victim to alienation if they feel like they cannot confide in the targeted parent. Allow them to speak freely and openly around you, and refrain from passing judgment or being overly hostile in response to how they are feeling. Make your home a space in which your child feels safe and secure and show them that they can come to you to discuss anything. This will also mean that you are privy to more of your ex's behavior and will know if they are speaking ill of you.

What NOT to Do if You Find Yourself on the Receiving End of Parental Alienation

Deciding to respond to parental alienation is a big step. If you do decide to do so, it is worth considering how to approach it and be mindful of whether your response could worsen the situation.

- Beg Your Child for Affection:

Resorting to begging your child to side with you is lowering yourself to the level of the alienator, and will only confuse your child further about whom they should trust, and how their parents are behaving. Avoid pleading with them to spend more time with you, try to win them over, or side with you against your ex. Try to avoid involving them in the situation at all where possible.

- Show Weakness:

Although you will undoubtedly be suffering, avoid showing this to your ex in any way, as this will only show that you are weak and that their alienating is effectively working. Remain strong and steadfast in your expectations and composure and present yourself as calm and put together when it comes to interacting with the alienator. Keep your feelings in safe spaces such as venting to loved ones or therapy. Equally, avoid showing the side of you that is terrified of losing them to your children, as an overload of anxiousness will cause them more worry.

- Withdraw From Your Children:

It might be tempting to reciprocate the feeling that your child is rejecting you by doing the same to them in return, either out of sadness or in an attempt to try and show them how it is hurting you. If they stop returning your calls and texts, avoid taking longer to reply to their messages, or mirroring their communication behavior. Be persistent when it comes to attempting to communicate with them. Do not overload them with texts, but check in on them regularly and remind them that you are present and that you love them.

- Forget you Have Authority Over Your children:

You are still a parent, not a friend or a peer. You are in charge of decision-making, and the responsible authority when it comes to your relationship. Children benefit from firm boundaries, and will likely respect you more in the long run if you set these and maintain your position.

- Try to Control Your Child:

It is a tricky balance because, at the same time as remaining in a position of parental authority, you need to not stray too far into trying to control your child. Avoid restricting their decisions or trying to force them to think in a certain manner, but instead encourage them to think freely for themselves. Attempting to force a certain way of thinking into your child or trying to control their allegiance will only be engaging actively with the alienator, and will likely turn this conflict into a larger and more turbulent war.

- Overexaggerate Every Situation:

It might be tempting to throw hands every time that your child comes home from their other parent's house a little sullen, or every time they roll their eyes at you or talk back. Not every little misdemeanor is related to alienation, nor worth taking a stand over. Take time to take a step back and reflect on what is and is not important, and trust your intuition when it comes to knowing when you need to intervene, speak with your child or your ex, or call on court-mandated support.

Involving the Court

If you cannot resolve parental alienation with your ex, nor with a mediator, you might need to escalate your situation by involving the court. This is typically done in severe situations, where you are unable to contact your child or illicit a response from them or your ex, and you feel at a loss as to how to protect your child from an ex who is working to turn them against you.

- How Courts Have Responded to Parental Alienation:

Being on the offensive is often the best approach when it comes to alienation. Involving third-party mediators, and when that is not enough, going back to court is often the best step to combat an aggressive alienator. This is where the importance of thorough documentation comes in as if the day comes when you require court intervention, you will be thankful if you have concrete proof of every and any interaction you have had with your ex.

Often, courts will order that family members attend therapy, and will request specific amendments to the parenting plan such as forbidding parents from defaming one another, and strict orders about how each parent is to communicate with the child. In cases that are proven to be severe enough, the court might request modifications to the parenting plan which give the alienated parent more time with the children. However, some cases have shown that preventing children from seeing the alienating parent if anything worsens the situation as the children become distressed from not being able to see the parent that they side with.

Unfortunately for the victimized parents, children can choose not to abide by court-ordered mandates and can still often side with the alienator; although there have been some attempts to force coercion, such as withdrawing child support for the alienator.

- How to Prove Parental Alienation:

You need to be able to show that how your ex is behaving is negatively affecting and causing harm to your child. This can be incredibly difficult, as you often have to defend yourself and your character and demonstrate that your child does not hate you – which can be hard if a child has already been alienated and is showing signs of rejecting you.

To prove parental alienation is happening, speak also to other individuals in your child's life, like teachers and coaches. Witnesses can often testify to behavioral changes and demonstrate if a child has been alienated, and has begun to act differently or favor one parent inappropriately.

- How to Disprove Parental Alienation:

If you find yourself being unfairly accused of parental alienation, ask yourself first if you might be unknowingly engaging in naive alienation. If this is the case, ask your co-parent what it is that you have done to make them feel this way, and try to pinpoint changes that you can make to let your co-parent feel more supported in your child's life. This can include speaking about them more favorably, encouraging your child to see them, or praising your child for a trait that they share with this parent.

A 2020 study analyzing cases of abuse or alienation showed that in cases where fathers claimed that mothers were alienating their children, the mothers had their custody revoked in 44% of the cases. In the cases where mothers were accusing fathers of alienation, they only had their custody revoked 28% of the time.

In the cases where mothers claimed that the fathers were abusive, the mothers were twice as likely to lose custody in cases where fathers countered this claim by saying that mothers were engaging in parental alienation versus where the fathers did not claim alienation, showing that alienation is generally trumps abuse (Meier, 2000).

Reintegration Therapy

Parental alienation cases that get taken to court often have reintegration therapy (sometimes known as reunification therapy) issued to the family. It is a therapeutic approach designed to rebuild the bond between an absent or alienated parent and a child.

Reintegration therapy is generally set over an extended period and tailored to each case. A qualified reintegration therapist meets with the family and allocates the parent assignments to help rebuild trust in the relationship with their child. This can include discussing a previous conflict to work on communication skills or playing a game together to provide positive interaction and reduce the feelings of negativity surrounding the alienated parent.

How to Heal From Parental Alienation

Recovering from parental alienation takes a great deal of strength and time. Although it might be your ex masterminding the operation, it is your child who is delivering the incredibly hurtful actions and words, and actively rejecting you. It can therefore be difficult to find the strength to fight for your custodial rights and your place as a parent if you feel overly spurned and alienated. However, it is important that you still fight for your rights. This involves consulting with a family law attorney and proving that you are a victim of parental alienation and then getting a good lawyer on board who knows the subject and can prove your case in court. Doing so might be difficult and time-consuming, but it is worth reminding yourself at every step of the way that this is in the best interest of your child, even if they are unable to see it at present.

Remind yourself that your child still loves you. Even if they are acting out against you or withdrawing, remember that they too are a victim of alienation, and are caught up in a storm of emotions and manipulation.

Additionally, you need to acknowledge that parental alienation is an incredibly hurtful and traumatic experience. Work on building a support network that you can rely on to discuss your own emotions. You will likely also benefit from seeing a mental health professional to discuss your experience with feeling rejected and abandoned by your child, as well as any other feelings such as shame, grief, and hopelessness. This will also help you channel some of the negative emotions you might be feeling toward your child elsewhere, so that you do not lash out at them, or your ex, and will help you avoid giving the alienator any fuel to use against you.

Looking After Yourself

Being on the receiving end of a crusade held by a parental alienator can be exhausting. You are likely watching your child suffer at the hands of someone whom you used to trust who is now trying to turn them against you, and feeling powerless in being able to protect them.

You might be experiencing some issues of your own, such as depression, anxiety, or post-traumatic stress disorder (PTSD).

Make sure to look after yourself in whichever way this means for you. If your mental health begins to suffer too much, you will be even less able to ward off the attacks from an alienating parent or do much to protect yourself or your child. Where possible, confide in loved ones about your struggles to share the burden, and attend therapy or counseling if that is also an option to try and help you navigate parental alienation.

Reflective Questions

1. You feel like your child has been withdrawing from you. They have not responded to your texts all week. How do you respond? Do you continue to reach out?

2. You notice that your child has been acting differently around you. They seem unhappy about having to come to your house and mention that their other parent has made negative comments about you. How can you bring up this topic with them and discuss what has been said?

3. You feel like your child is slipping away. They are constantly angry at you, disinterested in spending time with you, and beg instead to stay with their other parent. What is the next step? At what point do you involve an attorney?

Summary

In this chapter, we have explored what parental alienation is and what signs you can look out for if you are worried that your ex is working against you to brainwash your child. You will also be more informed about how to respond to signs of parental alienation, when to involve the court, and how to look after yourself if you do find yourself the target of parental alienation.

In the next chapter, we will explore 'What to do when …' and give you an overview of how to respond to situations you might personally be facing.

Chapter 8:
What to Do When

"As long as you continue to react so strongly to them, you give them the power to upset you, which allows them to control you."

— Susan Forward

Often, it can be a lot quicker to get things right the first time around. That might not be possible, but hopefully, with this book, you will be on the right track in knowing how to respond to certain situations. I, for one, was a bit lost when it came to getting back on the dating bandwagon. I was worried about what my daughter would think and avoided it altogether for the first few years after my divorce. Finally, I met someone. He was calm, kind, and gentle, even with my little girl.

I had dropped my ex a message when I felt that things were moving along nicely, and I had found that he slotted well into my life. I wanted to introduce him to our daughter. He was livid and told me I was out of my mind and in no way allowed to do so. I was selfish for moving on. I had probably been sleeping with strangers throughout our marriage. I was vain and vindicative and he would let all the world know that I was unfit to parent if I dared try to introduce them.

My daughter had occasionally come home and told me about a few women who swept through her father's apartment during their shared weeks. Initially, I tried to probe her for more details. Realizing how this trapped my mind in a negative cycle of thinking about these strange women, wondering what they had that I did not, spending my mornings staring into a coffee comparing myself to willowy made-up women in my head was not helping anyone. The next time she provided me with a snippet of information about one of these dalliances, I politely told her that Mommy did not need to hear any more about Daddy's life.

My ex, however, was less sympathetic. He would pry bits of information out of our daughter, and send me angry messages about how I was letting men slip in and out of our house in the middle of the night, putting our daughter at risk. He painted me as a woman at night, risking our child's safety for my pleasures. It was hardly aligned with the reality, which was my reliable boyfriend of nearly a year playing board games with my daughter, and helping with her school projects. I had been careful about introducing her to him. I had brought up the topic of mom's new friend almost a month in advance and explained how, after a divorce, two people can move on without hard feelings and find a new special someone who makes them happy. However, despite me gradually easing them both into contact with one another, my ex was still not happy to see me move on or to have someone else in the presence of our daughter. He calmed down eventually though. Despite the occasional disparaging comment or grumble when he dropped her off, we both allowed one *another to move on with our lives.*

Looking back, I would have done it differently. I would have set out exactly how and when my ex and I would introduce partners. I would ask that we both inform the other before doing so. I would also make a strict rule about no adult sleepovers whenever our daughter was visiting. Lastly, I would have stopped myself from asking about anything my ex was up to. I realize now that in doing so, I prevented myself from moving on for a great deal longer than was necessary.

When Your Ex Refuses Access

As a parent, you should naturally want to see and spend time with your children. If you suspect that your ex is behind preventing you from seeing your children, you should educate yourself on your visitation rights, and who you can turn to, to help you gain access to your children.

- **What Are Your Visitation Rights as a Parent?**

Courts generally deem that all parents have visitation rights, as long as this does not harm the children. They also recognize that children tend to benefit from ongoing relationships with both parents. This means that even if you do not hold full custody or live with your child, you will generally have some form of visitation right unless you are deemed to pose a danger to your child's well-being.

- **Court-Ordered Visitation**

Visitation rights and parenting time will depend on the custodial arrangements from your divorce, and whether the custody is shared or if one parent holds primary custody. Judges can also offer temporary custody orders for a divorce which is in progress.

You can also agree and settle on parenting arrangements yourself outside of court, although this will be unable to be enforced by the court.

Unmarried parents can also request custody. This will require a paternity test to prove parenthood if the parents were not married when the child was born or conceived.

Why Your Ex Might Be Withholding Visitation

Consider why your ex might be withholding visitation. Even if the reasoning seems futile and irritating, perhaps even upsetting for you, trying to understand why your ex is doing so can help you strategize your next move most effectively.

- They are unable to let go of your past together and move on.
- They are trying to punish you through your child and blame you for the divorce.
- If you are not paying child support and they want to force you to do so.
- They believe that you are a bad parent.

What to Do if Your Ex Is Not Following Your Parenting Plan

If you start finding that your ex is not following the visitation arrangements set out in your parenting plan, and either denying you visitation or ignoring your plans, do not panic. There are various steps you can take to make up your own parenting time, and then escalate the situation if required.

- Attempt to Make Up Missed Parenting Time

If you find that your ex only sometimes refrains from allowing you to see your child when it is your turn, you should have elements in your custody arrangement and parenting plan that set out what happens next. This might include an extra week at your house. If your plan does not directly cover what happens in the case of missed parenting time, you can try and agree on what to do with your co-parent directly, if you think that they will be cooperative.

- Mediation:

If your ex refuses to cooperate with making up missed parenting time, you might need a third-party mediator to help you come to some form of agreement. This might include counselors, therapists, or neutral custody mediators.

- Court-Enforced Custody:

If you have not been able to resolve making up missed parenting time either by speaking to your co-parent or through mediation, you can escalate your situation to the court. Approaches will vary across states, but you might be able to file for enforced custody orders by demonstrating that your co-parent is violating your custody agreements by withholding visitation. Judges will typically order parents to obey their parenting plan agreements and set out makeup parenting time. Repeat offenders might face changes to their custodial arrangements, fines, or even jail.

- Change Your Custodial Arrangement:

You can request a change in your custodial arrangement and argue that your ex is failing to follow your parenting plan and denying you visitation. Significant changes to custody will require you to demonstrate that this is in the best interests of your child, and only in severe cases will judges typically transfer sole custody to one parent.

- Call 911 in Case of Emergencies:

Police typically do not involve themselves in custody disputes unless the court has issued an order that allows them to enforce custody, for example in the case of a parent repeatedly denying visitation who has already been flagged. However, if you think your child is in danger, or are worried that your co-parent is thinking about kidnapping your child and taking them out of state or country, you should contact the police immediately.

Court Involvement

One parent cannot stop another from seeing their child unless they pose a threat to the child's well-being. This means that even if a parent does not show up for their child as agreed, refuses to pay child support, or breaks their parenting plan in any other way, visitation will generally not be denied by a judge.

A parent can, however, return to court to request limited contact or a cease in visitation. The latter will generally only be issued in extreme cases, where it is in the best interests of the child that they no longer see the parent in question.

Limited Contact

- Supervised Contact:

Rather than a complete cease in contact, judges might issue supervised visitation between a parent and child. This might be issued for parents who have certain behavioral issues such as alcohol or drug abuse, but do not pose an immediate threat. It might also be issued for parents who have not been in contact for an extended period and require a slow and supervised reintroduction to their child.

Supervisors might include trusted relatives, friends, or qualified professionals.

- Contact From a Distance:

If the situation is severe enough, a judge might order alternative methods of contact between a parent and a child that are not face-to-face. These might include texting, calling, letters, or emails.

- Made-to-Measure Solutions:

As every situation is individual, judges can issue creative solutions for each case. This might include stating that a parent can only see their child one day of the week, that they may not smoke in front of the child, or that they need to find accommodation closer to the parent that holds physical custody.

When Your Ex Is Badmouthing You

Children are easily influenced, particularly when it comes to hearing or overhearing what their parents say. If they do hear one parent criticizing another, they often struggle to lack the judgment to form their own opinion and might find themselves easily swayed, even if these comments are false accusations. Constantly listening to one parent badmouth the other can also lead to a great deal of emotional distress in children, who might not want to be involved, or start to feel guilty or anxious about how to position themselves in the conflict.

Badmouthing can come in all shapes and forms. It can range from being called names or insulted, to grand fabricated stories placing a person in a poor light. It can be "Daddy is so stupid with money, that is why we got divorced, why he lives in a small house, and why you cannot have nice things." It might also be an elaborate campaign and a false narrative about how a parent secretly despises a child and does not want to see them.

Types of Badmouthing

Badmouthing can come in all types and forms but generally involves one or more of the below elements.

- Name Calling:

This might include a parent using insulting and degrading names for their co-parent in front of a child, asking the child to call them by their name, or saving their phone contact as such.

- Blame:

A parent can badmouth another painting themselves as the victim of the other parent's misdeeds, such as saying that they caused the entirety of the divorce, or that they are to blame for financial issues shared by both parents.

- Lies:

Whilst everyone has their version of the truth, parents can turn to lies or distortions to support their badmouthing. Hearing lies from the mouth of a parent can cause children a great deal of emotional distress and display poor role model characteristics, which might increase their tendency to lie.

- Criticism:

Jumping at the chance to point out a parent's mistakes and berate them for it is an additional form of badmouthing, and often damages how the child sees that parent and their relationship with them.

How Badmouthing Affects Children

If you find yourself up against a co-parent who is badmouthing you or your children, consider the negative effects this has and where possible, try to intervene as early as possible to prevent these issues from taking root. Additionally, consider the potential consequences if you feel tempted to ever engage in negative verbal criticism.

- Relationship Impact:

Easily influenced children will soon come to believe the negative words coming from one parent's mouth concerning the other. They might start to become angry and resentful toward the parent who is being criticized, mimicking the behavior of the parent doing the criticizing. They might equally become angry with the parent doing the badmouthing, and lash out at them in an attempt to protect the parent who is being badmouthed.

- Loyalty Conflicts:

As explored in Chapter 6, loyalty conflicts can arise from frequent badmouthing between parents, forcing children to choose sides and causing them a great deal of emotional stress in the process.

- Poor Self-Esteem:

A product of two halves, children might take the criticism and badmouthing personally, and see it as an attack upon their character.

This can lead to them feeling the burden of these negative statements and suffering from feelings of negative self-worth as a result.

- Behavioral or Mental Issues:

Increased stress from hearing one parent badmouth another can lead to behavioral or mental issues in children such as anxiety or depression.

How to Respond to Badmouthing

If your co-parent is engaging in badmouthing, consider your response before retaliating or letting your emotions get the better of you.

- Do Not Let it Dictate Your Response:

When hearing someone speak negatively about you, it might be tempting to rush in to defend yourself or start sending jabs their way in retaliation. However, reacting to these thoughts in the heat of the moment is often detrimental in the long run, as it can lead to you acting impulsively. Engaging in badmouthing on your part in response will only confuse and stress out any children left in the middle, and will provide them with poor role models on both sides.

- Stay Calm and Composed:

As hurtful as hearing badmouthing might be, stop and think, how much energy do I need to give to this person, with whom I no longer share my life? What sort of role model am I setting for my children? It might be difficult to compose yourself, particularly if your ex is attacking your triggers and sore spots, but try to maintain your confidence and self-esteem, and avoid letting it overwhelm you. Additionally, if you hear negative comments from the mouths of your children, do not panic. Respond in a cool and neutral manner, and show them how badmouthing is a negative trait that impacts people, and how they can best respond when someone they love is being criticized. You should not be asking your children to defend you in front of your ex – instead, equip them with the necessary tools to combat badmouthing and protected loved ones in later life.

- Intervene When Necessary:

Depending on the severity of the situation, you can step in and ask your ex to stop badmouthing you. Avoid involving your children or asking them to relay messages to do so. If you are unable to communicate with your co-parent or find them uncooperative, consider asking a third-party mediator to step in and help you both find methods to put an end to the badmouthing.

Tips for Dealing With Badmouthing

When responding to your ex badmouthing you, avoid engaging in the following responses that might inflame the situation.

- Avoid Bringing in the Past:

Maybe your ex cheated on you or gambled away the money you were saving to buy a new house. Maybe they gaslit you, lied, or accidentally killed the family cat. None of this is relevant when it comes to your children, and how they see you both post-divorce or separation. They need so much support and reassurance instead of having to spend their time working out which parent is the bad guy, and whether their parents are lying about one another. When it comes to allowing your children to have a relationship with their other parent, leave the past behind and allow them to build a future.

- Do Not Retaliate:

Do not sink to the level of your ex by badmouthing them in return. Children listening to both parents degrade one another will begin to feel their world crumbling in on them. Instead, demonstrate your strength and moral character by staying calm and collected, putting your own emotions aside, and your children first.

- Empathize With Your Children:

Being stuck in the middle of parents fighting is a terrible crossroads to be at. Children will likely be feeling guilty about having to side with or defend parents, and struggling with loyalty conflicts. They love both parents and watching both loved ones hurt one another will only cause them increased distress. Show that you understand and are willing to listen to your children's feelings about badmouthing or being caught in the middle, and present a safe space for them that does not involve cussing your ex.

- Do Not Defend Yourself in Front of Your Children:

Particularly if your children are the ones presenting the

badmouthing, it might be tempting to quickly snap back and defend yourself in their presence. Avoid doing so, as like retaliating, this drags them unwillingly into a battlefield of who is right and wrong.

- Focus on Your Parent-Child Relationship:

Instead of putting your energy into retaliating or defending yourself, work on spending quality time with your child and nurturing your bond with them. Verbalize your care, show physical affection, and tell them that you will love them no matter what.

Responding to Negative Communication From Your Ex

If you are in a situation where communicating with your co-parent is difficult, set an approach in your mind as to how to acknowledge and respond to that person if they do end up sending you hurtful or insulting messages.

Ask yourself first if the message or call concerns your children. Does it impact their current well-being in some way? Or are they just dragging up issues from your shared past to hurt you? If it is the latter, the message will usually not require a response.

Secondly, are they asking a legitimate question? If so, try to ignore any insults or petty remarks they might be sending and respond only to questions that require it.

If you find yourself inundated by messages which are only worsening the situation for you both by heightening the conflict, consider moving to a reduced standard of communication, or removing it altogether. There are numerous online resources such as apps available to allow co-parents to organize themselves and their children without actually speaking to one another.

Dealing With Arguments

If you do find yourself engaged in arguments with your co-parent, be aware that disagreements are a part of life. Allow for some flexibility in not seeing eye to eye on issues, and be prepared to allow for some wiggle room on your end to accommodate their expectations, whilst expecting that they do the same in return.

However, unresolved disagreements might come back to haunt you, so try to get this cleared up as quickly as possible to avoid letting them impact your children's lives. Set out any resolved points in your parenting plan, to avoid future conflict on these areas.

Consider also how you communicate in these disagreements. Try to control your impulsivity and avoid reacting emotionally. Instead, work on your composure through mindfulness and react as calmly as possible.

Improving Communication

If communication is an area of conflict for you, consider how you can improve your style of communication to avoid arguments with your co-parent.

- Set Boundaries:

Set out everything in advance in your parenting plan, including how and when you will communicate, and the tone you can take with one another. The best approach is to treat your ex like a business partner. Be formal and appropriate, and avoid sharing or asking about personal details, or asking for anything beyond what one would ask for in a professional setting.

- Begin Sentences With 'I'

People tend to respond better when they do not feel called out or attacked. Positioning yourself in the fore frame of your words can assist in avoiding your ex feeling riled up and attacked, and then refusing to cooperate any further. For example, instead of "You keep telling Matt he can have a puppy and then not buying one for him. He is really upset and getting angry at me thanks to you letting him down," respond with "I know you told Matt that you would buy him a pet a while ago. I can understand why you have not done so since it is a lot to take on, but do you think we could work on not getting him excited about things that do not end up happening? I think he would benefit from some more consistency in his life."

- Use Active Listening:

When in conversation with your co-parent, practice your active listening skills by giving them your full attention, making eye contact, asking questions, and paraphrasing what they have brought to you back to them to show you have been listening. Avoid ignoring genuine issues your co-parent raises, but show that you are willing to listen and work with them to improve.

- Be Consistent:

Whatever communication standards you do set, be consistent with them. Avoid ignoring their calls and messages, but try to find a middle ground where you do speak more than once a month about important issues concerning your child

Communication Quick Tips

In review, keep the following pointers in mind when engaging with your ex to avoid sparking any unnecessary conflict.

- Treat your co-parent like a business partner.
- Listen and engage when needed.
- Do not use your children as messengers.
- Do not argue in front of your children or badmouth your ex.
- Accept your situation and your co-parent.
- Vent to your support system when needed.

When Your Ex Sabotages Your Parenting Time

There are several ways in which your co-parent can begin encroaching on your parenting time. This is generally divided into the following:

1. Direct Interference:

    - Your co-parent cancels your visitation time or drops your child off late.
    - Your co-parent takes your child during a visitation period allocated to you.
    - Your co-parent takes your child out of state or country without telling you.

2. Indirect Interference:

    - Your co-parent badmouths you.
    - Your co-parent refuses to let you speak to your child.
    - Your co-parent asks your child to spy on you.

How to Handle a Co-Parent Who Is Not Following the Plan

If you find that your ex is engaging in one or more of the above signs, consider your response. Gather yourself instead of acting emotionally, and compile documentation showing how your ex has violated your agreement.

Firstly, try and prepare for any violations of your parenting plan in the plan itself. Set out what happens if one parent were not to comply with visitation and the consequences for doing so.

Initially, when the issues arise, you may try to present your co-parent with the problem and ask them to begin cooperating and complying with the parenting plan.

If they remain uncooperative, consider escalating the situation to court. Be aware that leaving things too long may lead to a loyalty conflict if you are no longer in regular contact with your child, so acting quickly is often a good option. Involve a mediator, and if they too are unable to solve your issues, escalate the situation to court and request a change in custody arrangements or enforcement of visitation time.

Stepparents and New Partners

Hopefully, you can get to a point where both you and your ex move on from your separation and find fulfilling new partners. However, whilst a child should love a stepparent, a stepparent should never replace the love of a biological parent (if that parent is present and willing to engage with their child).

If You Feel Like Your Ex Is Trying to Replace You

Feelings of jealousy when a new partner is brought onto the scene are normal, but remember – you are all adults. The role of a stepparent is in addition to biological parents. If that stepparent is a healthy addition to your child's life and is caring and nurturing, take a step back and reflect on why you might be feeling jealous. Generally, these feelings will be down to your insecurities. Putting these aside to allow your child to form a healthy attachment to a stepparent is usually a move in the right direction, even if it hurts a little bit. It is however the best move forwards in the long run, as accepting your ex's new partner will reduce conflict and any chance of your children feeling guilty about accepting them in your defense.

How to Co-Parent With New Partners

If you have not already introduced new partners to your child, think about how you can do so in a way that minimizes conflict and keeps everyone as comfortable as possible.

- Set Out How and When to Introduce New Partners in Your Parenting Plan:

Communicate with your ex when it comes to introducing new partners to your children, and what a good time to do so is for both of you. You might have a set rule of at least 6 months of dating before introductions or a similar rule.

- Do Not Try and Stop Each Other From Meeting New Partners and Moving On:

Unless a new partner poses a threat to the children's well-being, you should not try and stop your partner from moving on with their life and finding someone new. They govern their future, and you will have no control over whom they date. Even if you are unable to meet the individual, try and have faith that your ex has your children's best interests at heart and would not bring anyone inappropriate into their lives.

- **Avoid Criticizing Your Ex's Partner:**

You might not love him/her, but avoid talking about your ex's new partner in a negative manner – particularly in front of your children. They will be easily influenced and swept up by your opinions, and this might cause the beginnings of a loyalty conflict if they feel like they need to choose sides.

- **Set Boundaries:**

To avoid feeling like you are being replaced, have some boundaries set out in your parenting plan or in agreement with your ex as to what new partners can and cannot do. For example, no overnight stays at the house alone with your children.

Introducing a New Partner to Your Children

When the time comes to introduce a new partner, try and set certain expectations with your co-partner as to how to do this in the best interests of your child.

- Avoid dating and introducing partners straight after a divorce and focus instead on your children.

- Prioritize your children, not your partners, especially soon after a divorce. Leaving your children feeling like they are in second place will cause feelings of resentment and anxiousness.

- Do not have adult sleepovers during your parenting time. Children will feel confused and upset if they see strangers (not long-term partners) sleeping over and leaving your house.

- Tell your ex when you do decide you are ready to introduce your partner to your children. Avoid letting your children relay the news, but instead, tell them in advance yourself so that they have time to process the news.

- Continue to respect your ex. If you are in a setting together with your new partner, avoid showing them off or engaging in too much public affection. Be mindful of old feelings and how your ex might be responding to seeing you with someone new.

How Does the Court View New Partners?

Whilst major life issues such as medical care and education are considered necessary to be shared between parents, introducing new partners does not fall into this category. Therefore, it is unlikely that there will be any way to enforce limited visitation between your children and your ex and their new partner, or vice versa. However, if the new partner poses a serious threat to the children, this can be escalated to court.

"My Kids Hate My New Partner!"

It can be very difficult to move on with your life if you meet someone new, but find that your children take an active dislike to this person. Maybe they voice this aversion by ignoring your partner or making snide comments in their presence. Maybe they glare at them over the dinner table and refuse to pass the salt. Maybe they avoid coming over on the weekends, making their dislike very clear. Having children take a stand and show very open resentment toward a partner can make having a relationship incredibly difficult. How you respond to a child in this position is difficult, as there is a fine line between balancing your child's needs and requirements against your own.

How to Respond to Children Rejecting Your New Partner

If you do start to feel like your children are taking an active dislike to your new partner, do not panic. You do not have to dump them on the spot. The reasoning behind your children rejecting a new partner might involve issues below the surface, so it is worth first trying to get to the bottom of this and gauge why your child is feeling this way.

- Find the Real Issue:

Your children might not actively hate one specific partner. They might decide to reject every potential new love interest. It is therefore important to find the real cause of the issue and determine if their dislike is down to your new partner's behavior, or if they are reacting to emotions resulting from the divorce; they feel threatened, left out, protective of your ex, or otherwise overwhelmed with so many life changes they cannot fathom another person coming into their life. If your child does suggest that your partner is flawed in a way that you have not noticed, it is important that you take this seriously and explore what might be making them feel unsafe.

- Talk to Your Child:

If your child is showing signs of actively disliking your partner, try and communicate with them as to why this might be. Be open to what they say, even if it is not what you want to hear. If they are not sure how to explain how they are feeling, encourage them to ask you questions about why you are dating and about your new partner, and explain to them the qualities in this person that you like and why you have chosen to include them in your lives.

- Try and Include Your Child:

A big reason behind rejecting a new partner is often the fear of being left out. Particularly after the upheaval of a divorce, children often feel unsteady about where they belong and if they are still loved. A new love interest on the scene can be viewed as a rival for what seems like a very precarious source of love and affected. When the time comes, you might try and include your child in some of your activities with your partner, to allow them to bond. Avoid doing so early on in your relationship as forcing a new partner on your children during limited parenting time and leaving them with a babysitter might increase feelings of loneliness and resentment.

- Allow Your Child to Set Their Boundaries:

Maybe your child does not want your partner sleeping over more than 3 days a week. Maybe they do not want them coming to their school play. Maybe they do not want your partner to hug them. These are very valid boundaries that you should encourage your children from setting. Allow them time to foster a relationship with your new partner, and do not force them into anything prematurely.

- Discuss With Your New Partner:

If the conflict between your child and your new partner is visible, do not leave your new partner in the dark to deal with it. They are likely feeling uncomfortable and unwanted as is, so be sure to include them in your discussions about how your child is behaving and how they can best respond. Healthy partners will respect a child's boundaries and have patience in integrating themselves into their lives – any signs of overstepping or making a child feel uncomfortable are often red flags in behavior.

- Involve Your Ex (if appropriate):

Although this might not always be possible in the case of toxic exes, you might be able to speak to your ex regarding involving someone new. If your child is rejecting a new partner out of fear and guilt for their other parent, you might be able to voice this concern and ask them to show their support, to alleviate these feelings of guilt and show your child that it is okay for them to accept someone new.

When Your Ex Undermines Your Authority

Ideally, your co-parent and yourself should bolster each other up from afar and support one another's parenting. You might however find, particularly in the case of toxic exes, that this is not the case and you instead have a parent who is actively working to undermine your authority.

- Parental Alienation:

A toxic ex might try to undermine your role as a parent completely through badmouthing, undermining your authority, brainwashing, and false accusations.

- Permissive Parenting:

One parent might break any rules and expectations set out in the parenting plan by allowing their children to do as they please, thus making them favor the more lenient parent over the stricter one.

- Doubting Parental Abilities:

A toxic parent might challenge the other parent's ability to parent, calling them a bad parent, abusive, or other negative accusations.

- Lying:

Children are easily influenced by their parents and will lose a sense of what is reality if they are constantly exposed to lies and mistruths. Toxic parents might use this to their advantage to undermine a parent and gain a child's favor.

How to Respond to an Ex Undermining Your Authority

Before jumping head first into retaliation or acting without thinking, consider the following steps when faced with a co-parent who is undermining your authority:

- Avoid Power Struggles With Your Children:

Your house, your rules. You set how your child behaves in your home, but do not control how your ex parents. Avoid engaging in emotionally charged arguments about what your children can and cannot do, and why everything is not fair. Your children know you very well and know also how to push your buttons and set you off more than most people. Work on learning how to calm yourself before jumping into conflict and responding whilst your emotions are at a high, and take a step back to compose yourself if needed.

- Avoid Punishing Children for Your Ex's Behavior:

You might be tempted to overreact to your child acting out after being told to go to bed early after being allowed to run wild at your ex's house. Try and look at the bigger picture and remember to take into account if your ex is undermining your authority and impacting your relationship with your child. Avoid also using extreme punishments and use appropriate consequences for bad behavior to avoid your children feeling bitter.

- Intervene When Necessary:

If you do feel like your ex is unsettling your relationship with your children and working to actively undermine your authority, consider speaking to your ex about how to resolve this issue, or escalate it to mediation or court if necessary.

Are You Undermining Your Authority?

You might be unknowingly undermining your authority with your children. It is easily done, but sometimes it is also hard to realize that you are also the root of the problem. Raising your voice, yelling, and responding to every situation with extreme emotions can detract from the real focus – your child's behavior – and undermine your response.

Equally, being too lenient in your boundaries can cause your children to lose respect for you. Stay firm and do not negotiate about important things to provide consistency, and know when to allow for your child's input and allow some wiggle room.

Finally, avoid rescuing your child. It can be hard as a parent watching your child struggle with tasks and you might be tempted to jump in and complete it for them. However, this teaches them that they can give up easily and will likely lead them to feel like they can fall back on you and throw in the towel when life is too hard. Help them out, but be prepared to let them work things out on their own rather than coming to their rescue at every opportunity.

When Your Ex Manipulates Your Child

We explored signs that your ex is manipulating your child in both chapters about toxic parents and loyalty conflicts, and the dangers of what happens when this happens without intervention. Signs that your ex is working against you that you should look out for include:

- Badmouthing you in front of your children
- Using your children as messengers to relay badmouthing or hostility
- Arguing in front of your children
- Lying about you and making false accusations
- Criticizing your parenting skills
- Interfering in your communication with your child by monitoring or preventing calls and texts
- Emotionally manipulating your child by making them feel guilty or ashamed about spending time with you
- Intruding into your parenting time by dropping off late or canceling
- Keeping you in the dark when it comes to important updates about your child

How to Respond to Your Ex Manipulating Your Children

If you do feel like your co-parent is engaging in the aforementioned behaviors and your children are at risk of being manipulated by them, avoid reacting immediately to the situation without thinking about how this might impact your overall relationship with your children and co-parent.

- Avoid trying to retaliate and manipulate your children in return.
- Provide a safe space where your children can share with you how they feel without judgment (active listening).
- Avoid arguing in front of your children.
- Encourage your child to think for themselves.
- Accept that you cannot change your ex.
- Document every interaction with your ex, in case you need to escalate it to court.
- Avoid rising to your ex if you feel like they are trying to trigger you.
- Do not blame your child for your ex's actions.
- Be kind to yourself and practice self-care.

When Your Ex Harasses You

Harassment involves extremely abusive and degrading communication. It is a step up from badmouthing, and can often be incredibly hurtful or concerning. You might find yourself barraged with a constant stream of verbal abuse attacking your character and your parenting. Often, the individual harassing you has some form of ulterior motives; they want to take out their feelings of anger about your divorce on you, want more control over your children, or want you to stop asking them for child support.

Types of Harassment

Harassment comes in many forms and involves repeating intimidating behavior and targeting an individual to threaten or scare them. It can range from:

- Verbal abuse, ranging from criticizing your parenting, your character, your appearance, your parenting abilities
- Making up and spreading false accusations to people in your close circle
- Name-calling
- Gaslighting
- Involving your children in the attack on your character
- Spreading rumors and harassing you online

Harassment is a big deal, as it can impact your relationship with your children and your own mental health and well-being. If you think your ex is engaging in harassment, try to set firm boundaries about what you will and will not allow. Avoid engaging in communication with your ex if this instigates harassment unless necessary for your children. If the situation is severely impacting your life, gather proof and involve an attorney as it can impact your custodial arrangements. Avoid retaliating in any form of harassment as this will worsen the situation. Take a deep breath, block them on social media, and try to find mindfulness tactics to keep you calm and composed if you do receive or hear about something hurtful.

When Your Ex Cyberbullies You

We share a great deal of our lives online. A toxic ex might use this to their advantage to defame your character, by posting hurtful images or statuses about you or messaging people you know with false accusations. They might create fake accounts to cyber bully you anonymously, try and hack your accounts to gain personal details about your life, or even stalk you using GPS tracking devices to gain information to use against you.

If you do feel like your ex is engaging in cyberbullying behavior, do not engage or retaliate. Convey to your ex that you know they are behind this, and ask them to stop. Do not respond or engage with posts but instead take screenshots and track the behavior to use later. Report fake accounts, change your passwords, and be conscious of cyber-hygiene to avoid letting your ex access your accounts any further. If there is a risk that the cyberbullying might escalate into physical abuse, or if you are otherwise worried for the safety of you or your children, report the behavior to the police and involve the court to enforce an end to it if necessary.

When You Feel Like Your Child is Abandoning You for Their Other Parent

Now well-versed in parental alienation, you should be able to look out for the signs of a co-parent who is actively trying to turn your children against you and force them to pick a side that is not yours. If you do think this is the case, and feel like your children are being manipulated into rejecting you as a parent, take a deep breath and consider your actions before you respond.

- Do Not Take it Personally:

Your child might be rejecting you for very valid reasons. Stay open-minded to this fact and try and identify if there is a legitimate issue at hand. Maybe they are going through a rebellious phase and find you overly strict. Maybe they dislike your new partner. Maybe you are visibly struggling to deal with the divorce and have not been able to dedicate to them the time that they need. If however, you are certain that the above does not apply and, knowing your ex, you can tell they are trying to maneuver your children against you, do not take it to heart. These are simply the actions of a malicious individual who is acting out in favor of their selfishness and is not a product of your character or flaws. Do not let it impact your self-worth or how you identify.

- Do Not Show Weaknesses:

As hard as it is, screaming, crying, or begging will all prove less fruitful in the long run compared to keeping your cool and responding with measured neutrality. Do not let your ex or your child show how much you are being hurt, or try to bend over backward to get them to come back to you.

- Do Not Fight for Your Children's Approval:

You might be tempted to enter into emotional conflict with your child by guilt-tripping them into spending time with you or trying to control them to pull them away from your ex. Doing so will only detract from your strength of character and your position, so avoid overly emotional or heated pleas.

- Show Up for Your Child:

Even if they prove resistant to communication and seem unwilling to engage, persist appropriately. Do not bombard them with messages, but remind your child that you are present, willing to listen on topics that might even hurt your feelings, and empathize with what they are struggling with themselves.

- Remember You Are Not Alone:

Parental alienation and being rejected by a child are incredibly hurtful. Being turned away by your child might at times break your heart. However, know that you are not alone in your situation. Countless have experienced the same. Support groups online might be able to offer you solace, and family courts also have experience in dealing with similar situations should you need to escalate your case.

When Your Child Refuses Visitation

If you have managed to set up and agree on a parenting plan, yet find that it is your child who does not want to follow it, it can be incredibly hurtful. Try and reflect and ask yourself why they might not be wanting to visit you during your allocated parenting time.

- Are you trying to enforce overly strict rules in your house?

- Do you live far away from your child's school and friends?
- Are you going through a period of high conflict and taking it out on your child?
- Does your child not like your new partner?

If you do conclude that the answer is one or more of the above, communicate with your child to try and identify if that is the problem, and see if you can find a solution that works well for both of you. Involve your co-parent, if necessary, as courts tend to encourage the involvement of both parents and might involve themselves if it is apparent that your ex is behind visitation issues.

If it is not your ex encouraging your child not to visit you, but an underlying problem, create a safe space where your child can talk about these feelings with you. They might indeed be hurtful and not what you want to hear, but refrain from passing judgment and lashing out at your child. Acknowledge how they are feeling and be empathetic to their situation. Reiterate to your child that you love them unconditionally and want to be there for them as a parent and that the presence of both parents in their life is important. Reflect on what they say and if there is anything that might be causing them to feel unwilling to spend time with you, that you could work on.

If you feel like it is your ex who is withholding visitation, there are certain steps you can take to legally enforce it instead.

- Enforcing Visitation Through Contempt Proceedings:

You can try and enforce visitation by applying for an order to show cause (OSC), demonstrating that your ex is withholding visitation and breaking your agreement. It will likely require repeat occasions where this has happened, with proof that your ex violated and withheld visitation on purpose. Judges might issue fines or penalties for initial offenses, before escalating your case to enforce a visitation order to allow you to see your child.

- Modifying the Custody Arrangements Because of Visitation Withholding:

You can also request a change to your current custody arrangements citing visitation failures and your ex's unwillingness to let both parents be present in your child's life.

You might, unfortunately, find that even despite the set visitation time, your child does not want to see you. They might be the ones refusing to come to your house or to get into your car. When this happens, document the incident so you have a record of what happens and can pinpoint what might be causing it. Next, try and communicate with your child and see why they are unwilling to see or spend time with you. If this proves unfruitful, and you suspect your ex of parental alienation or other forms of manipulation, involve a mediator or escalate the situation to court.

When Your Child Feels Ashamed

Divorce shame is common in children of divorce. They might feel guilty about having caused their parents to separate and might blame their bad behavior or think that their parents do not love them enough. Shame can manifest as grief, sadness, anger, or many other emotions, and lead to behavioral and mental health problems, so it is important to be aware that your children might be feeling guilty or ashamed so you can keep an eye out and help them navigate these feelings should they arise. Maybe if they had eaten their vegetables, Mommy and Daddy would still be together. Maybe if they had gotten better grades, Dad would not have left. The feelings can be consuming, and you should be ready to explain the reasons behind your divorce and help take the weight off of your children's shoulders.

Equally, if you are not working through your divorce shame, this can bleed out into your children. Perhaps you are blaming yourself for the divorce, saying you could have done better, been a better wife or husband, that you are a selfish and bad parent, that in getting divorced you have messed your children up for life. Put time aside and seek counseling, if possible, to help you navigate these feelings, so you can also help your children process the same feelings and are less likely to impact their feelings with your own.

What to Do if Your Child Is Struggling

Be mindful that even though your head might be clouded with sadness and grief and anger about the dissolution of your relationship, your child is probably experiencing many of the same emotions. Work on how to deal with these yourself at the same time as helping your child with how they can do the same.

- Try and Reduce Family Conflict:

Avoid arguing in front of your child and keep any divorce or co-parent-related concerns out of their sphere of influence, so they have less to worry about.

- Help Your Child Work on Stress Management and Anger Management:

Teaching your child emotional skills to help them manage their stress and shame and divert their anger elsewhere will help them ground themselves and prevent them from engaging in negative behaviors if they feel overwhelmed.

- Reiterate That You Love Your Child:

Remind your child that you will love them and that you are there for them. Feeling safe and supported can help alleviate feelings of shame or worry.

- Be Present for Your Child:

Demonstrate your love by being available to your child, whether it is for texting or calling or making sure you give them all of your attention and turn off any outside distractions during your parenting time. This will help them work through any shame or guilt over the divorce and ease into their new life.

- Prioritize Your Child:

Do not let negative behaviors develop in your child without your knowledge. You no doubt have a lot going on, but keep them a priority and make sure you always have their best interests at heart.

- Involve Your Child's School:

Shame can take many forms. Your child's grades might be dropping as they struggle to concentrate at school, or they might be partaking in bullying as an outlet for their anger. Communicate with the school if you are worried about them as teachers will be able to keep an eye on your child and alert you if anything happens.

Reflective Questions

1. You suspect that your ex is making fake accounts and sending your social media followers nasty messages about you. What is your first response?

2. You have a clear parenting plan that specifies that you have parenting time every other weekend, but your child texts you to tell you that they would rather stay with their other parent. How might you respond? Do you insist that they come to your house as planned?

3. Your children tell you that your ex is seeing someone new. You are angry because your ex has not told you about introducing this individual to your children, and they claim

that the partner is spending a great deal of time with your children – sometimes being left to babysit them. What do you do? How do you bring up the topic with your ex?

Summary

In our final chapter, we have hopefully provided you with solutions in many situations that you might face in dealing with co-parenting issues. You should have a better idea of how to deal with your children taking a dislike to new partners, how to respond to children that seem unwilling to see you during your visitation time, how to respond to being harassed by an ex, and what to do if you think that your ex is actively working to undermine your authority and manipulate your child.

Whatever your situation, in purchasing this book and moving to educate yourself on co-parenting, you have shown a willingness to learn and improve yourself. Even if you do not think that you fit directly into any of these scenarios, you can hopefully take some pointers as to how to respond to your issues in co-parenting with a toxic individual.

A Heartfelt Request

Dear reader,

I truly hope that this book has provided you with valuable insights and practical strategies to navigate the complex journey of co-parenting with a difficult ex-partner. Your well-being and that of your children are of utmost importance. As you continue on this path, you may wish to help others who are facing similar challenges. By sharing your genuine and honest opinion of this book on Amazon, you can guide other individuals toward a resource that may offer them the support they need during their co-parenting journey. As an independent author, your feedback plays a crucial role in the success of my book. I would be incredibly grateful if you could take a moment to write a review on Amazon when you have the opportunity. Rest assured, I will personally read and appreciate every single review. Please know that I value all feedback, be it positive or negative, and I am eager to learn from your thoughts and experiences. Thank you for your time, and I look forward to reading your review. Warm regards, Tiffany.

Scan to leave a review

Conclusion

Congratulations on finishing *Co-parenting With a Toxic Ex*. Whatever your situation, I am hoping you can leave feeling more informed about difficulties that can arise in parenting with a toxic co-parent, and confident in how you will personally approach any problems that might arise or have already risen in your life.

I hope you also leave feeling less alone. Divorce and separation are incredibly challenging, especially when you have children to think about. Nonetheless, you are not alone. Although it might feel like an extremely lonely and worrying time, there are millions of other parents out there in the same position as you.

Building a new life and finding what works for you in parenting with an ex is not always easy nor linear, but you will now be well on your way to knowing how to set out parenting plans, deal with toxic co-parents, how to spot parental alienation, how to respond to children who seem unwilling to spend time with you or appear to hate your new partner, as well as many other scenarios. Whatever your situation, you are a step closer to building a new life and moving forwards with your journey in healing from a divorce, whilst giving your children the best chance at rebuilding themselves too.

About the Author

Tiffany Austin, a compassionate and insightful author, has gained recognition for her groundbreaking book, *Co-Parenting With a Toxic Ex*. Drawing from her personal experiences and deep understanding of the challenges faced by individuals in such situations, Tiffany's life mission is to empower and support those who find themselves navigating the complexities of co-parenting with a difficult ex-partner.

Before fully embracing her calling as a writer, Tiffany spent years dealing with the intricacies of co-parenting with a toxic ex. This experience, coupled with her empathetic nature, led her to realize the need for a comprehensive guide that could provide support and guidance to others in similar situations. Consequently, *Co-Parenting With a Toxic Ex* came into being.

In her book, Tiffany combines practical advice with emotional support, empowering readers to create healthy boundaries and foster positive relationships with their children, even in the most challenging circumstances. Drawing on her journey, Tiffany offers hope and reassurance to those who may feel overwhelmed or isolated while navigating the treacherous waters of co-parenting with a toxic ex.

In addition to her work as an author, Tiffany is a devoted mentor, guiding others through one-on-one coaching sessions, and helping individuals foster resilience, self-care, and effective communication skills in the face of adversity. Her insights on the subject have been featured in various media outlets and podcasts, sharing her wisdom with a broader audience.

When not writing or mentoring, Tiffany cherishes her time with her own family, which serves as a constant reminder of the importance of nurturing healthy and loving relationships. She is an avid reader, a lover of nature, and enjoys practicing yoga and meditation to maintain her emotional balance and well-being. Tiffany Austin is a shining example of strength, resilience, and compassion, dedicated to helping others thrive in their co-parenting journey.

References

Anderson, J. (2014). *The Impact of Family Structure on the Health of Children: Effects of Divorce.* Linacre Quarterly. 81, 378-387.

Augustijn, L. (2022). *Children's Experiences of Stress in Joint Physical Custody.* Child Youth Care Forum. 51, 867-884.

Brand, J., Moore, R., Song, X., and Xie, Y. (2019). *Parental Divorce Is Not Uniformly Disruptive to Children's Educational Attainment*, Proc Natl Acad Sci U.S.A. 2019 Apr 9; 116 (15).

D'Onofrio, B. and Emery, R. (2019). *Parental Divorce or Separation and Children's Mental Health.* World Psychiatry, 18: 100-101. https://doi.org/10.1002/wps.20590.

Darnall, D. (1999)/ *Parental Alienation: Not in the Best Interest of the Children.* North Dakota Law Review, Volume 75, 323-364.

Donahue, K., D'Onofrio, B., Bates, J., Lansford, J., Dodge, K., Pettit, G. (2010). *Early Exposure to Parents' Relationship Instability: Implications for Sexual Behavior and Depression in Adolescence.* Journal of Adolescent Health.

Maccoby, E. E., Buchanan, C. M., Mnookin, R. H., & Dornbusch, S. M. (1993). *Postdivorce Roles of Mothers and Fathers in the Lives of Their Children.* Journal of Family Psychology, 7 (1), 24–38.

Stafford, M., Kuh, D., Gale, C., Mishra, G., Richards, M. (2015). *Parent-Child Relationship and Offspring's Positive Mental Well-Being From Adolescence to Early Older Age.* The Journal of Positive Psychology 11, 326-337.

Wallerstein, J., Lewis, J., & Packer Rosenthal, S. (2013). *Mothers and Their Children After Divorce: Report from a 25-year longitudinal study.* Psychoanalytic Psychology, *30* (2), 167–184.

Winston, R., Chicot, R. (2016). *The Importance of Early Bonding in the Long-Term Mental Health and Resilience of Children.* London J Prim Care (Abingdon) 8, 12-14.

Printed in Great Britain
by Amazon